T0123355

The Will to Write

Select Published and Unpublished
Works of Reg. B. Cornejo

Reg. B. Cornejo

authorHOUSE®

AuthorHouse™
1663 Liberty Drive
Bloomington, IN 47403
www.authorhouse.com
Phone: 1 (800) 839-8640

Published by AuthorHouse 10/10/2019

ISBN: 978-1-5462-7224-3 (sc)
ISBN: 978-1-5462-7223-6 (hc)
ISBN: 978-1-5462-7222-9 (e)

Library of Congress Control Number: 2018914731

Print information available on the last page.

Any people depicted in stock imagery provided by Getty Images are models, and such images are being used for illustrative purposes only.
Certain stock imagery © *Getty Images.*

This book is printed on acid-free paper.

Bible version used is The World English Bible (WEB) which is in the Public Domain

I want to dedicate this book to my parents for believing in me, my wife, and all of my teachers and college professors who each inspired me in their own way to fulfill my dream and become a writer. I also dedicate this book to William Shakespeare, Edgar Allen Poe, Sir Arthur Conan Doyle, and Herb Caen of the San Francisco Chronicle my muses.

Preface

To MY READERS, I WANT to first thank you for spending your hard earned money to buy this book that has a collection of my published and unpublished works that spans my life time of writing. Some of the stories are news articles that I wrote for various types of magazines, newspapers, or journals. The other works consist of fiction and non-fiction short works or stories that I just never got around to sending in to publishers because my life took me in another direction. Finally, I have also decided to include some of my published and unpublished poems that I first wrote for my own pleasure but later decided to share them with my friends and the public. I want to take the time to thank Suzanne Lopez-Isa of The Hispanic Outlook in Higher Education and the other publishers who gave me permission to use my works that were published in their publications. I will note these articles when I use them in my book.

Before I get ahead of myself, I want to tell my readers a little story that I feel will help them understand why I decided to write. The story was told to me by my parents later in life when they noticed I had decided to become a member of our school newspaper. According to my parents, one day after spending the day shopping for groceries they decided to put me on the floor near the table where they were unpacking the groceries. When they got to a small box that had been filled with canned goods, they threw the box on the floor and continued to put away the groceries. When they finished their task, they looked down and watched me pull the box towards myself, pick up a crayon, and then put round circles on the bottom of the box. According to my parents, I then proceeded to start tapping on the circles (like I was typing on a typewriter). When they stopped me and asked me what I was doing, they said I responded by saying, "I am writing a story." I guess I should add that according to my parents I had just turned five years old, so I guess I knew I was going to be a writer from the day I was born.

Before I allow my readers to start reading my book, I want to note here that the first selection found in this book is one of my favorite short essays or stories that I wrote for a wonderful magazine/newspaper that is published in the Southern California beach town of Ventura, California. I selected this story because I wrote this work to be read not only as a news story but also as short story feature work. I once read that Washington Irving said "he would never be bound by rule; that he liked, when telling his stories, to linger by the way, take his time, and embroider his narrative as he pleased" (Tucker, Marion Samuel, Ph.D. editor, <u>The Man Without a Country and Other Stories.</u> Hale Edward Everett. The MacMillan Company, New York: 1920.). And, like Mr. Irving, I too often like to bend the rules without breaking convention. I hope that this first story will push my readers forward and inspire them to read the rest of my book with an open mind and an open heart.

First, I want to add a little more information about myself that might help my readers understand me better and know me better. Like the spirit of Christmas present said in the movie/book <u>A Christmas Carol,</u> "Come in and know me better, man." Anyway, first I want to say that when I was in college my works not only got published, but I was honored as a participant with an invitation to participate in the California State Arts Faculty Exchange, that according to the Faculty leaders "is the only program of its kind in the CSU system that was established in 1991." I want to add that the Exchange is "an opportunity for CSU Arts Faculty to share ideas and participate in stimulating discussions, and be directly involved with the internationally acclaimed CSU System Arts festival. Although it was a great honor, that same year I graduated with my MA from California State University, Bakersfield and was offered a chance to teach English at a private college on a part time basis. Since I needed to pay back my school loans, I of course took the job and went to work and decided to not participate in the Art's Exchange.

Finally, since I am a Native American, I have often been asked to do lectures about my culture and I have always accepted because I love the chance to tell people about who Native Americans really are so they won't see us as just stereotypical icons from the past. An example of one of my chances to lecture on my people's culture came when I was teaching college as a full-time junior college professor (non-tenure track one year contract) for Oxnard Junior College (Oxnard, California). This chance came on March 11, 1998 when I was allowed or honored to be part of the Oxnard College Scholar's Series. On this date, I spoke on "Native Americans: Demystifying a Culture." My lecture consisted of speaking on the thoughts and customs of the American Indian," so I could try to educate Americans on who my people were, and are now in the 21st Century.

Now that my readers know a little more about me, I present my readers this book that includes some of my published and unpublished essays, stories, and poems that have a little piece of me, and I feel they let the public see a little part of my soul. I hope my book both entertains you and teaches you a little bit about how a modern Native American thinks and sees the modern world around him.

I want to make one more point before I allow my readers to enjoy my essays, stories and poems of this book. I found a profound statement in a book that was written by President John F. Kennedy and published in his book titled Profiles in Courage back in 1955. I am going to use President Kennedy's short statement as a quotation because I feel this statement captures the essences of why I write and refuse to be silenced. This quote is the reason I wrote some of my essays and stories that are found in this book and the reason I wrote my controversial book In Defense of the Constitution: Ending America's Occupation and decided to update and republish it in 2019 along with my latest book that you hold in your hands:

"It takes great courage to do what you think is right even though it may mean the end of your career and the dislike and criticism of your friends and neighbors. Many people never have the opportunity to show such courage. But all of us have the opportunity to recognize such courage in others, to respect the person who is doing what he believes to be right even though we think he is wrong... [This] is a lesson to all of us that courage is much more than bravery on a battlefield...it can mean acting according to your beliefs whatever the consequences. And it is also a lesson that we can all share in such courage by refusing to join with those people who make unreasonable attacks on the man who is doing or saying what he honestly believes to be right" (Kennedy, John F. Profiles in Courage. 1961. Harper and Row, New York and Evanston.).

Note: All Photos in this book by Reginaldo Cornejo

"Native American"

In God's Image I was made.

Nurtured in His Garden of Love,

Delivered by my father's aid

I live in peace with God's dove.

Allied with Nature to live as one,

Never to forget I'm an Indian's son.

Nah-Kee-Teesh
Aka: Reg. Cornejo

Ventura County Reporter

Condor Mountain

Published June 12, 2003 in the Ventura County Reporter as a main feature story.
I now offer its reprint for your enjoyment.

This Condor is one of the lucky Condors who is now on the mend thanks to the staff of the Sespe Condor Sanctuary near Ventura, California. When this Condor is better he will be released back into the wild.

Ventura County Reporter

Condor Mountain

Published June 12, 2003 in the Ventura County Reporter

"In the Los Padres National, the search for a condor chick reveals a powerful metaphor for life in the balance, and of all—hope. Story and Photos by Reginaldo "Two Stones" Cornejo" (Intro by the Reporter)

By Reginaldo Two Stones Cornejo

W E ARE PERCHED ATOP A flat dome that rises 3,500 feet above sea level in the Hopper Mountain National Wildlife Refuge complex, home of the California Condor Recovery Program. Scanning the large southern ridge of the Sespe Condor Sanctuary, we look for sight of the California Condor, indigenous to this area.

On this warm spring day around noon, there are no condors to be seen, just a lone raven soaring on the warm thermal updrafts that linger over the cliffs and attract the condors. Still, although the condors are feeding and not around, a spiritual quality permeates these sacred mountains. Covered with Native American petroglyphs, these mountains have been the home to the California condor since the Pleistocene era (10,000 – 100,000 years ago).

The objective of the professionals and volunteers of the Hopper Mountain Ridge is to maintain and protect this prime roosting and foraging habitat for the endangered birds. Situated six miles north of Fillmore, California, the 2,471 acre refuge is home to about forty wild condors whose small population now includes a new chick. The hatchling has refuge biologists excited, and they have instituted a "round-the-clock" watch to protect it and its parents—without making to much contact.

According to Mike Stockton, the supervising wildlife biologist of the Sespe Sanctuary, the chick was discovered on May 9 or 10, 2003. "The Chick is at its most vulnerable stage right now," said Stockton, "so we don't know what is going to happen." Stockton has every right to worry. "Last year three pairs of condors also mated in the wild but all of the baby chicks died at the age of five months. We thought they were all going to make it; they were so close to the fledgling age of six months but they all died right before they were able to fly," added Stockton. "We checked them out and found that one had bottle caps and other pieces of garbage in its stomach that were found around the nest, but we could never find the cause of the death of the other two," concluded Stockton. Stockton explained that condors are prone to eating bone fragments to help with digestion, so biologists think the adult birds might have mistaken the garbage for bones and brought them into the nest.

To avoid any problems with the newest chick, Stockton and his team informed me that a team of biologists entered the nest and sifted out the garbage. "We hope to avoid any of the problems of the first three chicks and give this one some help," said Stockton. Part of this assistance centers around making sure that the condors do not know that humans are helping them. "If they did know," Stockton pointed out to me, "they would immediately become dependent upon human aid." According to the biologists, the recent nest clearing was a carefully orchestrated maneuver, as are the frequent carrion deliveries and all of the surveillance of the condors.

While we were waiting for a condor sighting, Stockton received a call from one of the many volunteers who maintain watch over the nest. The Volunteer informed Stockton that the parents were about to trade places. "Good," Stockton said, "they are doing what they are supposed to do." According to Stockton, the condors take turns eating for them-selves and feeding the baby chick. The parents, I learned, will feed until they are full then return to the nest to feed the chick, who eats almost around the clock.

While Stockton felt good about the chick's parents performing their proper duties, he added that for every biologist who felt captive-raised condors could mate and raise chicks in the wild, there were just as many who felt they couldn't succeed. "Those people who doubted their (the condors) ability don't understand that mating and raising chicks comes naturally to these birds," said Stockton. And with a smile, Stockton added, "No one has to teach them that (job)."

As I interviewed the staff, I learned the chick's parents were two young condors. The male condor, referred to as 125 because of his tag, is an eight year old who had never mated, while the female, number 111, is a nine year old who had mated the year before but had lost her chick. All of the condors are named for their numbered tags; they are also fitted with radio transmitters that allow biologists to track them.

A quarter of a mile away from one of the many feeding sites in the compound, my host and I looked through binoculars to see condors picking at a carcass that was left at the site by a volunteer under cover of darkness. Stockton informed me the refuge team only uses frozen still-born calves to feed the condors because the still-born calves are free of any chemicals or hormones the dairies might give surviving calves. "The calves come from Bakersfield area dairies in Kern County California," said Stockton. "In fact, we have a team in Kern County right now doing a still-born calf run," added Stockton.

While I watched the condors feed on the dead calves, this scene made me realize these great birds were not much different than my ancestors who had been put on Indian Reservations and fed cattle instead of being allowed to hunt for their meals. This action was supposedly taken to protect my ancestors, because the land was needed for development and the changing demographics made it dangerous for them to be a part of mainstream America. For the condors, the Sespe Refuge appears to be doing the same job, but in a more effective fashion.

Still, mainstream society takes its toll on these condors. I say this because I learned that every once in a while "some trigger happy person shoots one of these magnificent birds for fun—as was the fate of a female condor last year— or some condor dies of lead poisoning from eating carrion polluted with lead bullet fragments left behind by a careless hunter. I should add the U.S. Fish and Wildlife Service biologists and volunteers are helping the condors return to the wild, and that is a good thing, but the fact that this is necessary makes me sad as an American. Unfortunately, as a country, it seems to me that we always wait until a crisis state arises before we take action to save our indigenous plants, animals, birds, fish, or forests from extinction.

On top of the sad conclusion I came to in my last paragraph, the American Government (and its politicians) has a record of periodically reducing funding to programs like the U.S. Fish and Wildlife Service to the point that its employees can't do their jobs. It appears to me these type of actions will be the case this coming year thanks to the Bush Administration.

It is too bad that these politicians do not understand that as we destroy our forests and extinguish one species after another, we are cutting the integral links from the chain of life that keeps this planet whole and alive.

Speaking from the viewpoint of an American Indian with the horror of near-decimation fresh in our mind and blood, I believe we humans move one step closer to extinction every time we decimate a species.

As a person who knows I am part of the great circle of life, or as I like to call myself Pnaci (an old Native American word for indigenous person), and as a someone who spent a day with Mike Stockton, I believe biologists think a lot like Chief Luther Standing Bear of the Oglala Sioux tribe. Standing Bear once said, "I am going to venture that the man who sat on the ground in his tipi meditating on life and its meaning, accepting the kinship of all creatures, and acknowledging unity with the universe was infusing into his being the true essence of civilization." We Americans can be grateful that we have active preservation biologists like Mike Stockton and his team who believe that being civilized means caring for the flora and fauna of this great nation and the world at any cost.

As I thought about all of the work that was going into protecting the condors and that one precious newborn chick, Stockton and I were suddenly surprised to find ourselves in the company of four or five soaring majestic condors who had come quite close to check us out. Stockton said that the condors are naturally curious by nature and possess incredibly sharp vision. "They can see great detail with their red eyes," he informed me. "That is how they find their food; they are also very smart. They know us by sight and can tell when something is different," added Stockton.

Stockton knew what he was talking about because the condors came so close that I could take their pictures and see the details of their feathers. As they circled above us, Stockton made a curious observation. He pointed out to me that some of the condors were from the Ventana Wilderness Sanctuary in Monterey County. "Yep," he said, "some of those birds are molting and you can see their wings are kind of beat up from the long flight here."

I took some photos of the birds and I noticed through my 135 mm lens that Stockton was right. The Monterey condors' wings had many missing feathers. They were also younger birds, smaller, and did not have the orange-red white wing markings of the more mature birds from the Sespe Sanctuary. As I watched the birds, I noticed all of the condors appeared to be equally curious about the stranger who was standing on one of their mountain peaks.

Then, as suddenly as they had arrived, the condors disappeared into the blue sky. I should note here that studies show condors can fly at 55 miles per hour and can soar as high as 15,000 feet in the sky. As I watched the birds, Stockton told me he often watched the condors perform this quick appearance and disappearance act: "You see a small dot in the sky, and before you know it, you see this huge condor approach you like a bomber in the sky," he informed me.

Stockton next took me to the ranch house that serves as the base for the refuge. Nearby is a rearing facility for young condors that are waiting to be released into the wild. Stockton pointed out that they always put an older bird in with the young ones so the older condor can teach them about surviving in the wild.

For those readers who are thinking about going to one of the condor release sites, I was advised by Stockton that the sites are closed to the public. He did add that sometimes arrangements can be made for educational visits or special groups, if done in advance. I was also advised that the Hopper Mountain facility was constructed in 1995 so it is relatively quite new, so things might change in the future.

As for the current job the Hopper Mountain facility is doing, I am happy to report the facility provides a naturalistic environment with six simulated nest caves and 30X50 foot flight pen where an electric pole provides aversion therapy to remind condors who will soon be dealing with a forest of power pole lines to avoid these posts and their lines. The site also temporarily holds injured or sick condors. I was informed when the condors get too sick to be helped locally they are taken to the Los Angeles Zoo animal care facility. "They are the best condor doctors," Stockton assured me with a smile.

Many things Stockton said and did convinced me that Hopper Mountain's newest addition to the local condor population is in good hands. Although the baby chick is still in danger, and will be through its young adulthood life, I am happy to say it is being looked after by many genuine human beings who know the value of a life. As a Native American I know that trying to be one with the world is not an easy job, but I am happy to say the rewards found in the job that help mother earth stay healthy are worth it, because mother earth gives back to us what we give her. This line of thought has always been a Native America ideal. We are all part of the web of life says my Native American heritage, so if we Americans (and the people of earth) continue to destroy small bits of the web of life, the entire web of life will weaken beyond repair and we will all parish.

The Note

By Reggie Cornejo

Island girl of the rising sun,
In the land of the taloned bird;
Hears the ruffle of wings that run;
Seek you the sound?
My voice you heard?
Nightingale, please seek the hawk.
Let lotus blossom set its roots.
Dear gentle lady please tame the hawk, the
      hawk that flies and never roosts.

(I wrote this poem after I completed my first teaching contract and had returned to the states. I wrote this because while I was in Japan I met a young man that had fallen head over hills for a young Japanese girl, but her parents would not allow her to marry the young man. I found his problem so sad that I ended up writing this poem in his honor back in 1999.)

The Hispanic Outlook in Higher Education

VIVA JAPON: Impressions of a Gaijin

Hispanic Professor Teachers ESL in Japan

Published July 14, 2000 in The Hispanic Outlook in Higher Education

Note: This article is being published with the gracious permission of the publishers of the Hispanic Outlook. I wish to thank Suzanne Lopez-Isa for her kindness and professionalism.

The few students on this photo are some of the Wonderful students of Shibaura Institute of Technology that made my stay in Japan seem like a Wonderful dream that I didn't want to end.

The Hispanic Outlook in Higher Education

VIVA JAPON: Impressions of a Gaijin

Hispanic Professor Teaches in Japan

"Although Most Japanese citizens can read and write in simple English, they have few skills in speaking English which is the reason I am in Japan." (Hispanic Outlook citation)

By Reginaldo Cornejo

THE THERMOMETER READS A PLEASANT 88 degrees, but the humidity, which is around 80 percent, makes it feel more like a Roman steam bath than a center court in the Japanese city of Shinjuku, a suburb of Tokyo. I've been in this heat for a little over an hour waiting for a meeting that just won't start. The humidity is doing strange things to my hair, making it curl up around my collar, and my mind is slowing to the point where I fail to see the beauty of Shinjuku's high tower district.

"Make a note," I tell myself. So I pick up one of the two notebooks I have decided to carry with me while I am in the land of the Rising Sun, and I start to write. I've been in Japan for about a month and every person, place, building, train, object, and food dish still catches my attention. I'm not your typical alien white-collar worker or Gaijin in Japan. As a matter of fact, I am not your typical English Instructor in this country.

"Explain it to them," my little voice urges me. But all I can think of are the quick notes I'm writing in my notebook, and this full slice of life I'm enjoying that would be fit for a king.

I'm enjoying the flavors of Disneyland, the Mad Hatter's tea party, and Pinxtos of San Francisco all at once. I look up and find that I'm still sitting in front of the Century Southern Tower Hotel located in the Keio Plaza. I'm facing or looking at a fancy bar/restaurant called Hiroshima. From what I can see, the customers are not couples but businessmen who drink beer after beer and act as though they are eating a light dinner. You could say they are testing the amount of alcohol their livers will process before they drink themselves into a funk (Did I say that?). I know this drinking ritual happens every day because I see these hard working Japanese men going home day after day drunk as, well (as we say in America) skunks.

Although these businessmen have captured my attention, I should admit that the small group of couples and young ladies also amaze me. They seem (or appear) to be social butterflies. To paraphrase one of my favorite writers/ authors: "They come and go like moths in the night that are drawn to the light." One can only wonder how many hours of work these people have put in, why they are still up at 9:30 P.M., and where they are going in the dark of the night. Before I move on, I should add that most Japanese employees work from 9 A.M. to 9 P.M. or 10 P.M. at night. With the sounds of trains and cars coming and going, the people continue to parade for my pleasure. They are unaware they are being documented and frozen in time for my personal pleasure in these notes.

Ah yes, the Japanese people so stressed and so caught up in the act of adopting Western ways yet they are scared to death that a Gaijin (foreigner) will come near them, look at them, or worse yet, talk to them in English. Although most Japanese citizens can read and write in simple English, they have few skills in speaking English, which is the reason I am in Japan.

As a native English-speaking teacher, I am a prized English instructor. My job is not only to teach EFL/ESL English but to make myself available to the students for "free talks" during the time I'm on my employer's college campus. I am never to speak Japanese to my students (not my job), but this rule of my contract does not apply to people I meet after work.

At the Cafeteria:

It's a Friday afternoon, and I am sitting at Shibaura Institute of Technology's cafeteria. Friday is a good day to eat at our school's cafeteria because it serves a good dinner for under Y1000 (yen) or about $10 US dollars (Warning: If you come to Japan, things are very expensive.). I've lost 17 pounds, if not 20. I am probably going to go home a little lighter than arrived. Japanese food seems to have that effect on most foreigners—I do not know why. "Get back to the people of Japan and teaching English," my voice tells me. I have never met a people so scared and/or shy of foreigners, but at the same time, in my opinion, so in a hurry to lose, destroy, and forget their heritage because they want to adopt Western ways to become a World Power. The Japanese public seems to be bent on doing everything it can to look and act Western. This quest can be seen in the changes being made to the culture, morals, clothes, physical appearances, television ads (Kevin Costner and Meg Ryan are hot in Japan), and the Ken and Barbie type foreign teachers that many K-12 schools, colleges, universities, and corporations hire to teach English in Japan.

To paint a clearer picture of this trend, I guess all I have to do is look across Shibaura's campus and describe the majority of my students. My college students dye their hair blond and use sunless tanning products to get fake tans. The young women (especially the high school girls) use blue eye shadow and purple lipstick in an attempt to look like Barbie for the young men who try to look like Ken, or pass for a reasonable facsimile of a Caucasian. These students are dead set on looking white to the best of their abilities (the richer ones even wear blue contact lenses), which makes no sense to me. I say this because, as a man of color with Hispanic and Native American Indian roots, I know that for the past 500 years Native Americans have been fighting to keep their cultural heritage alive in America, the melting pot of the world.

Tradition Eroding

Before this trip, when I thought of Japan, I thought of three-generation families in which children, parents, and grandparents lived together. I thought of traditional Japanese homes with floors lined with woven mats called tatami, and acres of rice fields. I also thought of a country and people who believe education is very important, that students should be seen and not heard, and that bowing is essential. But, I guess I was wrong because tradition isn't selling well in Japan anymore. I observed that most families in Japan have only one or two children in their households, and that extended family households are not so common. Traditional housing has given way to apartment blocks or "danchi." These high-rise apartment complexes have polished wooden floors, carpeting, and modern restroom facilities. My apartment has 29 floors and looks like any apartment complex in the United States.

But the biggest change in Japan appears to be coming from the young people. Looking at some of the Japan's junior high, high school, and college students, you would think they grew up in one of America's ghettos. That is, they have little respect for authority, don't want an education, and dress in whatever fashion statement they want to make. On school days, you can find junior high and high school aged students out shopping in the big cities or hanging around train stations with friends at 11 or 12 P.M. at night. Some high school students and college students don't even go home. They play all night and ditch school the next day.

Before I continue, I should add that many of the students I just described here are exceptions to the rule, but not all of Japan's students are going crazy with their new-found freedom. For every free-spirited student who is fighting the system, I learned there are at least 10 to 15 (my observation) students who are growing up with respect and honor for their country's traditions. I was lucky enough to meet and teach both types of students at Shibaura University.

The Teaching Experience

So what was it like to teach Japanese students in Japan? Well, after overcoming resistance from some students who had a problem learning English from an American who did not look like anyone on Beverly Hills 90210, I can honestly say it was rewarding and the time of my life. My students turned out to be hard workers who were not only interested in learning English from me but also interested in learning about my Native American and Hispanic cultures.

"Teaching my students that America isn't the land of Ken and Barbie turned out to be the best part of my job." (Hispanic Outlook citation)

As a multicultural person, teaching my students that America isn't the land of Ken and Barbie turned out to be the best part of my job. With each lesson, my students not only learned to speak English better, but they learned about America's other citizens. Each day, after their English lessons, they would ask me questions about Native Americans and Hispanic traditions. My best reward was watching them drop their resistance to being taught English by a non-Caucasian. Through me, they learned that America was more than McDonald's, blond haired men and women, stock markets, Chevy Blazers, and hot apple pie.

During my tenure at Shibaura, my students learned about Cinco de Mayo, pow-wows, empanadas, Indian Fry Bread, and what it's like to live in the U.S. as a man of color. They even learned a little about Mexican and Native American legends, or tall tales, if you like. These talks included discussions about the Native American church, shape shifting, Christmas, Christians, Spanish ("Yo soy tu Amigo/I'm your friend.), and Apache (Tah-in-hoon-ay-ish-lee/I'm your friend.). I felt it an honor to teach these students about other cultures in America.

I would like to give some advice to anyone who is considering teaching English in Japan. This adventure is not for the faint-hearted. Be ready for a life-changing experience. My employers recommended that I read <u>Culture Shock </u>by Rex Shelly (1996) or <u>A Japanese Mirror </u>by Ian Burma (1975). These books will help prepare you for the experience of a lifetime.

NOTE: This was not in the article but I felt I had to add the following details to prevent any misconceptions/misunderstandings about my Cultural background. Although I did my best to answer the questions about the Latin/Hispanic cultures the Japanese students asked me, I have to admit that I felt inadequate when I tried to explain the Cinco de Mayo holiday or other questions that pertained to the Mexican Cultural because I am American born and raised. I say this because my father's family has Portuguese and some distant Navajo blood in his family's background/ lineage and my mother's family is only one generation away from being full blooded Lipan/Mescalero and Navajo registered Native Americans. My family members are all registered and card carrying tribal members because of my mother's blood line.

Jamie

The running brook,
A glass of wine,

The way you look
Your hand in mine,

Soft rolling hill,
A drink of wine,

Time's standing still because you're mine.

Published in the <u>World Treasury of Great Poems</u> 1981

A Dreamer Comes Home

(Written for one of my undergraduate classes in the 1980s to fulfill a course requirement.)

A Dreamer Comes Home

Note: This short story was written to complete an assignment that was assigned for one of my undergraduate English classes. The story is fiction and it is pure make-believe. I say this because after my professor read it and graded it, she asked me if it was a true story. I hope you enjoy a break from reality.

Fiction by Reggie B Cornejo

WHEN I DROPPED OUT OF Canoga High School, I took the fist job I could find, selling shoes on commission in a small store near the main street in our town. I felt lost and my education wasn't helping me get any richer. It was time to sink my teeth into a real job. I was in a hurry to make my mark in the world, but I didn't really know where. I thought that if I could make it as a shoe salesperson for now, I might get an idea. Dumb, yes! Yet, as a child of the world, it was a profane view. I would come home feeling dejected and exhausted, the cloth on my knees of my pant's legs worn. I felt like a jerk. I did manage to make time for fun, and I always found enough energy to party and sleep around with girls I met at the store. It just seemed like the natural thing to do. The dates came so easily, and if I didn't do it now, when would I do it? The girls weren't anything special, but I was having fun, and it filled my time.

I read somewhere that all men are given a life constitution at birth and on this constitution is written their life and the goals they will accomplish. The only catch is that the man must reach for the goals to get his reward. So it should not have shocked me when the girl of my dreams walked into my life at the shoe store I was working in to earn a living. I had expected this kind of reward to come to me all along. She was beautiful and had alabaster skin, faultless features, and an impeccable sense of confidence. She was also very rich. I know it sounds too good to be true; but, like I said, it was part of my constitution of life. She wasted little time in trying to get my attention. I was only trying to sell a pair of shoes to a princess that was too perfect for a lowly shoe salesperson like me. I didn't even own a car. When I happened to look up, I caught her looking down at me; her eyes danced as they met mine. I was still trying to sell the shoes to make a buck. The minutes turned into hours as I fumbled for something to say to make the time pass faster. She finally spoke and to my amazement it was something that all young men hope to hear. She started explaining that her family had not always been so prosperous and that she would like to have me met them. She also added that she thought I was cute. I was flabbergasted by her remark. I decided right there and then to let my princess do all of the talking so I wouldn't make a fool of myself. As I fitted the princess with the shoe, I allowed her to keep doing the talking.

My princess then paused, and when she continued talking, she said she had decided to make me her special friend from the moment she had seen my smile. The princess then asked me if we could go out to dinner that night, and after that we could go dancing and drop by and meet her parents. Then, she added that next week she had planned to go on vacation, and did I think I could come with her? As I listened, the princess added that I just had to accompany her and she wouldn't take no for an answer. As she kept talking, she said her parents were sending her to Spain for two weeks and they would be meeting her there so it would be so much fun. She caught herself and then asked me if these plans were fine with me? I was so dazed I could only nod my head to say yes.

Was this young lady for real or was someone playing a joke on a young adult male who was just starting to mature in a cold and cruel world? Was this fast moving event all a dream? The angel continued to speak and then asked me if I thought I had enough clean clothes to make the trip? The next question from the angel was also rapid fire and caught me off guard because she asked me if I felt I could get permission from my parents (and work) because she needed an answer soon. Before I knew it, the princess had our month planned out, and all I could do was smile at her. I could only guess that when you are that well-to-do you felt you had the power to make such snap decisions that even affected other people's lives.

The pain seared through my leg, and I lifted up the leg I had been kneeling on, I found the cause of my discomfort. I had put my knee down on a small thumbtack. The Princess was still there, but she was now silent. The minutes again took their true value in time and space. I asked the Princes if I could get her any other shoes. I then also did my usual low-pressure sales pitch for some knee high stocking, and she kindly said no. The voice that spoke was now transparent and cold. I boxed the Princess' shoes, and the young lady followed me to the register. The pain from the pin was hot and I could feel the blood slowly fill the hole in my skin. The Princess was no longer interested in the shoes she had just purchased. Her mind was now motivated to find the perfect dress for the new pair of shoes she had just bought. I put the shoes in a bag and handed the Princess her credit card.

As I waited for a thank you, the Princess turned and slowly cantered out on life's highway, never turning back to see the young man left behind in the shoe store. The young man walked toward the large glass-plate window of the shop, and as he turned his eyes to the sky, he thought to himself, "looks like rain."

The Damaged Circle

By Reg B Two Stones, 1994

The town? It doesn't really matter.
The people just don't care.

It all just makes me sadder.
They don't really make it fair.

I am trash within their eyes,
Never good enough for them.

I hear in their cold lies,
Though they say I am as them.

It's in to be their color,
Not the color that is me.

I am; I yell and holler,
My country is of thee.

Note: I think this statement applies here and to my article:
"The secret of happiness is freedom, and the secret
of freedom, courage." Thucydides

The Hispanic Outlook in Higher Education

PUNTO FINAL!

"STEP OFF THE SIDEWALK"

Published July 28, 2000 in The Hispanic Outlook in Higher Education

Note: This article is being published with the gracious permission of the publishers of the Hispanic Outlook. I wish to thank Suzanne Isa-Lopez for her kindness and professionalism.

The Hispanic Outlook in Higher Education

PUNTO FINAL!

"STEP OFF THE SIDEWALK"

By Reginaldo Cornejo

"Reginaldo Cornejo is a graduate of the CSU System, has taught at College of the Sequoias in Visalia in CA, Oxnard College in CA, Santa Barbara City College, and Ventura City College in CA. He has been published in the San Francisco Chronicle Examiner, the Delano Record, the Native Magazine the Anicus Journal, and the Ventura Record to name a few publications..." (Hispanic Outlook Citation)

IT SEEMS LIKE YESTERDAY THAT my father and I were walking down that street in the New Mexico/Texas area of America and came upon several white men and a white woman on the same side of the sidewalk as we were. The event had occurred many times before, but this day was different, for it taught me a lesson about racial equality.

The men confronted my father, and using several profane words, ordered us to get off the sidewalk and, "...let a white woman pass." My father didn't move at first, so one man added, "Get off the sidewalk, Injun. Don't you understand English?" My father looked at me, smiled, and did as he was told. I now know that my father could have started a fight. He stood over six feet tall and was a big man (235 pounds), but I think he avoided a fight because of me.

I never forgot that day. Since my father had shown so much intelligence, I decided to take his example and use my brain instead of my fist to survive in a white man's world. I promised him I would go to college and get an education, and I did. Unfortunately, my education has caused me a new problem in the politically correct 1990s.

Having earned a double BA in 1983, and after working in journalism for more than six years, I found myself teaching adult education, and I enjoyed the job so much that I decided to return to college and earn a Masters, or MA, and become and junior college teacher. During and after my graduate studies, I taught at private colleges, adult ESL (to Spanish speakers), K-12 substituted, and worked as an adjunct and associate professor.

And after two years of applying for full-time tenure-track positions at all of California's junior colleges, I have learned that like my father I am being asked to step off the sidewalk to let America's white women pass again. The reason I have to step aside, I've been told is that men have suppressed women in America for so long that women should be hired over all men immediately.

This country is still predominately Caucasian and controlled by "white men." They hold all of the powerful positions in corporate America, and we have only had white men as Presidents (Note: This article was written in 2000 before President Obama was elected.). Having pointed out these facts, I have to say, historically, men of color were considered second-class citizens when compared to white women, so I have to ask, "When or how have "men of color" ever suppressed or oppressed white women in America?

The Answer is of course "never." Yet, in 1999, I find men of color, including me, being ignored and passed over to fill teaching positions with white women (and token women of color) because America's white brothers and white sisters have decided they are going to correct gender inequalities in America's hiring practices of the past at my cost.

I am currently doing a college-by-college study of California's junior college faculties (written in 2000), and so far, I have found that the majority of the schools are running 90 to 95 percent Caucasian.

I'm not angry—just sad that America has not grown out of its racial/bigoted and/or protectionist ways. The fact that we do not have affirmative action departments in some schools, like Cuesta College, and that some of California's junior college faculties are becoming nearly all white (Porterville and Cuesta College for example) only serves to expose thee real agenda behind the killing off of Affirmative Action in America, which to me is the fear of losing control of the best jobs in America and making sure that the high-paying jobs are protected for future white college graduates.

My take on this protection act is that America's minority males have become casualties of political correctness—an imaginative and successful game of political semantics that appears to have been created to control and suppress them. The message we get is that if minorities want to work in education they have to take the jobs that are made available to them by those in control. If they don't want these jobs, these powers say minority males can work in other fields.

Some people may find my statements in this article bold; however, I feel they pale in boldness to Francis Fox Piven's statement about the plight of the "low-to-lower" middleclass minority males (and to a point white low-to-lower middleclass males too) and their fight against those in power in 1970s America: "...the specter of ending up on 'the welfare' or in 'the poorhouse' makes any job at any wage a preferable alternative. And so the issue is not the relative merit of the work itself; it is rather how some men are made to do the harshest work for the least reward."

Note: This added comment was not part of the article, but in retrospect, I found that it applied here nicely: I can attest that Francis Fox Piven's statement rings true because when I found myself unable to find either a part-time or full-time job teaching at one of California's junior colleges, I decided to take jobs overseas in countries like Japan and Hong Kong, China and use my MA in English Composition with an emphasis in TEFL and TESL to teach English in these countries.

Instead of inserting one of my poems here, I decided to insert a facsimile of a letter I received from one of my muses that inspired me to become a writer. The letter was sent to me by the late and great San Francisco Chronicle's columnist Herb Caen after he read something I wrote and heard that he had inspired me to become a writer.

San Francisco Chronicle

September 21, 1995

Reginaldo, you are <u>good</u> and have every reason to feel pride in your work. If I helped in any way, I am pleased and flattered. Keep it up!

Herb

901 Mission Street San Francisco, California 94103-2988 (415) 777-1111

Note: About the same time I received the wonderful letter, I had applied for a writer's job in the San Francisco area and the assignment asked me to write about local points of interest in the Bay and San Francisco area. I decided to apply for the job, and the following article is what I decided to write as I traveled around the Bay and San Francisco area. I want to note that I used Mr. Caen's wonderful format that he used in his daily articles during the time that he wrote for the Chronicle. I pray I did his style and format justice, but no one can replace the original. No, I didn't get the job:

On the Run in the City

By Reginaldo Cornejo

On the Run in City

By Reginaldo Cornejo

OAKLAND IS A VERY LUCKY city, not only are they lucky enough to have their Raiders back in the city of Oakland, but they also have the Hampton Inn in their city. I make this statement and observation because during my recent stay in Oakland, I discovered the Hampton Inn of the fine city of Oakland, California. This great business not only provided me with accommodations for my stay in Oakland, but it also made me feel like I was part of the family, or a big wheel. Yes, the clerk did her job and checked me in and made sure I was treated as a guess; But! I feel this employee went a little farther when she found out why I was in town; I say this because she then gave me a special rate that I had not expected. However! the special service didn't end there because my stay only got better and here is the reason why it only got better: The rest of the staff seemed to go out of their way to make sure I had everything I needed to make my two day stay as comfortable as possible. I won't bother my readers with the details, but suffice it to say, I left this business knowing that I had just been served by a class "A" business. I don't know about my readers past experiences, but in these days of fast-food, one day meetings, faxes, texting, and cold, cookie cutter like businesses, this type of business with employees who go that extra mile are hard to find.

A Time to Train: I want to note that the Harbor Bay Health Club of Oakland recently hosted a United States Tennis Association (USTA) Clinician's training session. And, I was lucky enough to be a part of it and see these USTA trainers in action. The seven hour program was held on September 10, and the training program, I am happy to say, attracted both players and coaches from all over Central and Northern California. As I talked to the participants, I learned most of them had decided to attend this training session, or camp, because they loved the game of tennis, they wanted to help kids discover the game tennis, and they wanted to be future clinicians themselves. The session included both on-court and in-service training on presenting all of the United States Tennis Association's youth and in-school programs. I'm happy to report that many of the coaches were there because they like to help low-income or disadvantaged youths who usually never get a chance to learn to play the game of tennis. Who were these coaches? They were good people and coaches who care about America's future generations. The coaches were everyday people that came from many backgrounds like a dentist, a retired businessperson, recreation directors, and many people from all walks of life that just wanted to contribute and give back to their neighborhoods.

Coming around the bend: On my most recent trip to Santa Cruz, I discovered that visiting Santa Cruz during the middle of the week is a great choice. If my readers have the time, I suggest they take some time off from work and enjoy this area during the middle of the week. I suggest my readers have a middle of the week lunch, or a half day mini-vacation from the big city in the near future. If my readers take me up on this offer, I can assure my readers that they won't be disappointed. I know I can come to this conclusion because most of the businesses are open, and since it's the middle of the week, the businesses are usually slow so they go the extra mile to make sure they show their appreciation for your patronage. If my readers need a tourist fix (want to meet some people, or tourist, from other countries), I can assure my readers that you will find tourists in Santa Cruz even in the middle of the week, like the wonderful couple I met from Germany while enjoying a light breakfast. This foreign couple was a pleasure and joy to meet, and I was even taught a few new German words during our conversation. I hate to say it, but there is nothing like an espresso by the sea while enjoying the company of two great people.

Don't do as I do...: There is always one in the bunch that ruins the mood. The most recent T-Shirt that caught my eye and gave me a laugh during my trip to the bay area was spotted in the Salinas area. I had stopped in the Salinas area to get some dinner at Denny's when three cowboys who appeared to have had too much to drink came in and sat down in the booth next me. As I watched these three men sit down, I noticed one of the men had a T-Shirt that had the following message: "Dare to Keep Kids off Drugs." Believe me my readers, "You can't make this kind of stuff up." Anyway, as I ate my dinner, I couldn't help but laugh and think, "I hope he doesn't have kids." Will we humans ever learn?

Sarah's

Something special is brewing there;

A place where coffee turns the air,

Riding the breezes to temp the lips,

Always tempting, so measure your sips;

Have it with sugar or drink it plain,

Sarah won't rush you, don't even strain.

Note: This poem was written for a friend's cheese cake coffee shop that was located on Main Street in the city of Porterville, California. Sad to say, like the rest of many small businesses in California, it no longer is in business because of the costs of operating a small business in the state of California.

As stated at the end of the next article, professor Reginaldo Cornejo was the both the director and head coach of the Minority Youth Tennis Program of Porterville during its long run in the Porterville area. The program was paid for and sponsored by both the United States Tennis Association and many local Porterville Businesses who cared enough to give back to the community. This photo shows many area students who took advantage of the long running and successful program.

The Native Magazine

It's Our Call

Of Wooden Rackets,
Nature and Graphite

Note: This article was published in both the <u>Native Magazine</u> and <u>It's Our Call.</u>
I have decided to combine the two versions from the "Native Magazine" and
"It's Our Call" because I want to give the "It's Our Call" organization that prints
this publication the exposure it so justly deserves. The organization is titled the
Minority Participation Committee of the Northern California Tennis Association.
My article was printed in "It's Our Call" in the Fall of 1995, and The Native
Magazine in the Summer of 1994.

The Native Magazine

Of Wooden Rackets, Nature, and Graphite

By Reg Barroso Two Stones

I LEARNED A LITTLE ABOUT MANKIND and tennis from two unlikely sources this year. The sources were an article I found in the United States Tennis Association's membership magazine and an old wooden racquet from days gone by. Although the article pointed out bidders and collectors had paid $2.5 million dollars for the 86 pieces of "Big" Bill Tilden memorabilia that had been up for auction, I found it more interesting to notice that some of Bill Tilden's personal rackets had also been sold at the auction. This small observation on my part only served to remind me I still owned the Bancroft Bill Tilden All Star Racquet I had learned to play tennis with during my junior years.

"Reg Two Stones reflects upon the lessons learned from both his tennis and cultural pasts." "It's Our Call"

After I finished reading the article, I went out to my storage room to look for the forgotten treasure from my youth. I found the racquet buried under several boxes still wearing its old style wooden racquet press. Remember racquet presses? These wooden racquet presses kept the racquet's head from warping while in storage.

As I pulled the racquet out, I slowly took the press off my share of Bill Tilden memorabilia, and I decided to take a couple of backhand strokes. I was shocked to find the racquet felt like club. To my chagrin, I also found the leather grip to be hard and cold to the touch so I slowly put it down on the table in front of me. I then realized that like the rest of the world I had been seduced by today's modern technology and today's sports equipment.

As I looked over at my racquet bag that held my light graphite infused tennis racquets, I came to an epiphany. My sleek, graphite powered, black beauties with the "made in Taiwan China" label had changed me, or seduced

36

me. Sure, my graphite racquets were great racquets but these racquets had been designed by an unfeeling computer and made by machines. These racquets had no past or history and even the materials were man made and not natural. Yes! I had become a part of the imitation generation that used synthetic racquets in an imitation world that played a power-laden tennis game in the fast world of the 1990s.

After contemplating my realization, I then remembered something my American Indian grandmother had always taught me about respecting nature and her gifts to mankind. I remembered that when American Indians killed animals, picked berries, or cut down a tree, they prayed for them for giving up their lives to help us live on this earth. Basically, my ancestors prayed or thanked these living things for dying so they could live, or enjoy life. Since my Tilden racquet was made of wood, I decided it was worthy of the same respect.

Feeling better, I picked up the All Star Tilden racquet again. The racquet now felt like an old friend. I studied the grip, and I noticed its octagonal handle was more pronounced because of the wood slats used to create the angles. This feature made it easier to find my forehand and backhand grips. I also studied the rich gold colored wood stain on the fine white-ash and then I admired the layers of wood in the head. The throat bridge of the racquet had been reinforced with a red fiberglass material, which made it easier to note the shiny little inconspicuous decal which read, "America's Oldest Tennis Manufacturer Established 1882."

As I collected my thoughts, I suddenly realized today's tennis game is simply a product of today's technology. That is the game is a mating of money, computers, greed, and space age chemicals to a grand "old-game" that once had a heart and soul, and the new game that had has been created is a plastic and power-laden game that we see on television.

I realized my Bancroft racquet represented everything that tennis used to be, but had been lost to this modern, plastic world. Like my white-ash made racquet, the tennis game and its pros of the past had been a natural phenomena that had evolved naturally. Pros like Althea Gibson, Rod Laver, Helen Will Moody Roar, Arthur Ashe, Billy Jean King, and Bill Tilden had never attempted to be bigger than the game, but they had instead respected and nurtured it. They played a natural game with tools made from nature's kitchen, and the game was grand.

"Reg Barroso Two Stones is a Native American writer, educator, artist, and tennis coach who resides in Porterville, California. His Porterville Minority Youth Tennis Program was recently awarded a United States Tennis Association Star Search grant." "It's Our Call"

Peace

By Reggie B Cornejo

The Angel asked the Father,

"Is Mankind really true?"

The Father told the Angel,

"The answer's in my shoe."

A smile grew upon God's face as he wrote another page.

The Book knew of his grace and the word became the sage.

Ventura County Reporter

Art and Culture

Winds of Change: R. Carlos Nakai brings down the House

By Reginaldo "Two Stones" Cornejo

Note: This article was published in the Ventura County Reporter on May 15, 2003 in the Art and Culture section. I wrote the article to review the musical performance that was presented on the University of California at Santa Barbara campus by the renowned musician R. Carlos Nakai. I was later informed that the Indian Studies Department was so taken by my article that they enlarged it and hung it in their department's office. I thank The Ventura County Reporter for publishing my work.

Ventura County Reporter

Art and Culture

Winds of Change:
R. Carlos Nakai brings down the House

"Review" by Reginaldo 'Two Stones" Cornejo

V ENI, VIDI, VICI (I CAME, I saw, I conquered); William Shakespeare once wrote these moving and powerful words of prose for the character Julius Caesar: The words were written, or used in Shakespeare play, to show Caesar's self-determination to control his destiny and the power he had to inspire his followers.

Hundreds of years later, on May 8, 2003, these words could aptly be applied to R. Carlos Nakai a modern day Native American warrior/musician who came, saw, and conquered the stage and audience of the University of California at Santa Barbara's Lotte Lehmann Concert Hall with a performance that would have brought down the house at Carnegie Hall.

Nakai was nominated for a Grammy for Best New Age Album category on January 7. The nomination recognized Nakai's album, "Fourth World—one of 27 albums that Nakai has created under various labels—for its unique sound.

Nakai's performance was nothing less than inspiring. Using a variety of flutes and some modern-day-technology, Nakai melted the hearts and minds of his 21st Century, car-driving, burger-eating, West Coast audience. And then, he musically transported them into the canyons of the Southwest where they heard the streams cascade over the rocks, and in an ethereal way, felt the wind flow through their hair: At times the flute music was so captivating that some of the audience members would feel their primal spirit being reborn, and a yelp or primal grunt would come from one of them.

"Through my music, I will paint a musical picture for you that you can see in the canyons of your minds." R. Carlos Naki. (cited by the Ventura County Reporter")

During his dialogue, Nakai said that he "relied on research and innovation to recreate the sound of feeling the journey he was taking us on" (like the synthesizers and reverberation unit he used to recreate the echoes of the canyons where he created/wrote his music in Arizona). Nakai added, "We are all on a journey, and this unit and the flutes allow me to paint a picture for you so that you may see the journey I am taking you on."

After explaining how his system had evolved, he added, "Imagine, if you will, a large artist's canvas hanging over your heads that is ready to be painted on. Now, through my music, I will paint a musical picture for you that you can see in the canyons of your minds." And after making this statement, he did just that.

As a man with Apache/Navajo blood, I watched Nakai's performance as an insider. I not only felt the illusion Nakai created with his flute but I also felt 18th Century America before the Europeans walked the hallowed canyons that Nakai's flute and technology took us to in the music. I again felt the breezes and smelled the white sage growing on the land of my people.

Through Nakai's flute, I was able to hear the cry of the eagle and feel its freedom as it soared the skies of Indigenous America. Unfortunately, I also heard in Nakai's dialogue a man struggling to walk a fine line between being an Indigenous man/Native American and being part of the greater circle of life that is being an American in the 21st Century, as I do.

Nakai later added that he viewed each flute less as a musical instrument and more as an instrument to create sound art. He explained that the Northern tribes liked one sound pitch and the Southern plains Indians liked another sound. The sounds, or pitch, were either high or low depending on the tribes.

While Nakai educated his audience on the various flutes used by Native Americans, he also used many different flutes to play his music. He added the he liked to work with other musicians on collaborations.

Nakai's press release stated that although his classical training in the cornet and trumpet has influenced his music, it was "his curiosity about his heritage that led him to the play the flute, and in 1972, he took it up seriously." I'm happy to say Nakai has never looked back.

Jenny Lynn's

(1996)

By Reg. B Two Stones

Plano and Vandalia, where concrete, asphalt, metal, and time
did build Jenny Lynn's;

Simple elegance, not to be outdone, building offers drink to
some, but only the ones;

Join the crowds; it's up to you; enjoy the setting; it comes
with food, but only for some;

This is the dream built for some; sit with the tables that come
with chairs; watch the clock as it counts its time.

(This poem was written for a new restaurant that I had the pleasure of
being one of its first customers and because the service and ambiance
was so refreshing and special, I decided to write this poem to use on their
napkins. Sad to say, the new owners sold the business soon after it opened
and the magic left with them, so I just kept the poem and the memory.)

The Ventura Reporter

Good Neighbor Policy
NEWS

The Chumash Casino Joins the Ventura Chamber of Commerce

By Reginaldo Cornejo

(Note: This article was published on May 8, 2003 in the Ventura Reporter. Because I walk a fine line between being an American Citizen and a member of an American Indian Tribe, I wrote this article because I felt I could serve as a mediator to help all of the players that were for the project, and against the project, step back and look at this project through each other's eyes so they could address all the worries and questions this project had raised in a logical way.)

This photo of the Chumash Casino being built back in 2003
Shows how big and expensive the project was when it was finally
approved by the city fathers of Solvang, California.
As my readers can see, many area businesses profited
from this projects construction.

Ventura County Reporter

Good Neighbor Policy
NEWS

The Chumash Casino Joins the Ventura Chamber of Commerce

By Reginaldo Cornejo

I T'S A BEAUTIFUL DAY IN the city of Ventura, California. There's a slight breeze coming in from the ocean that rustles some stately palms that line the streets of Ventura. The palms towering over business and private homes provide a South-seas atmosphere that attracts tourists and visitors from all over the world. The Ventura Chamber of Commerce wants to market the charms of Ventura to an ever-wider audience, and for the most part, locals welcome outsiders and their tourist dollars, but the whole town started buzzing recently when word went out the Chumash Casino had joined the Chamber of Commerce.

The Ventura Chamber of Commerce, I should add, exists to provide member businesses many products and services that help them do more business in Ventura. Often when a major business chain or franchise is thinking about locating in a city like Ventura, one of the first steps these new businesses take is to join the local Chamber of Commerce like the Casino was attempting to do in this area.

I should add the Chumash Casino is located in the Santa Ynez Valley (quite a few miles up the road towards Santa Barbara, California), but they are currently expanding at a record pace so many Ventura citizens got worried that the Chumash Tribe was thinking about expanding into Ventura, a move that many citizens felt would increase area traffic and compound the current housing shortage in the area, and not to mention the more subjective objections many people have to gambling.

But does the Chumash tribe really want to turn Ventura into a West Coast Atlantic City? "Not to worry," says Gary Robinson the public relations manager for the Chumash Casino. "The Chumash tribe has no interest in expanding to Ventura. The Casino is just adding the city of Ventura's Chamber of Commerce to its growing list of other memberships that include the Buellton, Solvang, Santa Ynez, Santa Maria, Lompoc, San Luis Obispo, Santa Barbara, and Goleta Chambers of Commerce," added Robinson.

But what was intended as a PR move nearly became a public relations disaster. It almost became a disaster when the casino failed to explain its motives and the rumor-mill took over. According to Robinson, the Casino decided to become a member of Ventura's Chamber of Commerce, "... so as to serve our Ventura area customers better and contribute to their community."

When asked if he could provide an example of how the citizens of Ventura were going to benefit from the Casino's Chamber membership, Robinson said, "The Casino has already contributed to the Ventura County Search and Rescue team and we are currently looking at several other programs we can help."

As for fears of the expansion off the reservation, Robinson said that the Tribe had no such interest. "The Chumash Tribe is too busy working on its 200,000 square foot casino in Santa Ynez that will open in the fall of 2003." (Note: The Casino did open as planned and all of the fears and worries that local communities had raised appear to have been worked out by all involved; at least at the time I was writing this book in 2019.)

When I was writing this article in 2003, confusion about the nature of Tribal gaming was not limited to Ventura and it extended beyond the Ventura Chamber of Commerce problems and questions. First of all, I have to clarify that Tribal gaming is not a Federal welfare program, as some people may believe. The truth is that America's Native American Tribes initiated gaming for themselves to erase the poverty found on many American Indian Reservations, and they defended their right to create this means of support all of the way to the United States Supreme Court. I should add that many Tribal Governments have developed their gaming operations without any US Federal or state assistance. Because of the competitive factors, market conditions, tribe sizes, and geographic locations, the only negative factor these American Indian Tribes face is that some Tribes produce more income or revenue than others.

To help these Tribes, in 1988 Congress passed the Indian Gaming Regulatory Act which affirmed Tribal gaming as a legitimate tool for reservation development and Tribal self-sufficiency. Today (in 2003), about 200 of the Nation's 562 Federally recognized Tribes have gaming programs and they spend more than 212 million dollars annually to regulate their gaming operations and pay for both state and US Federal regulatory costs.

Most Tribes realize they have their work cut out for them if they are to convince the public that Indian Gaming is good for not only the Tribes, but all of America. Cultural barriers, lack of understanding, and misinformation (like the fear generated when the Chumash Casino became a Ventura Chamber of Commerce member) will continue to be a problem for these Tribes, but if the Tribes continue to provide hundreds of jobs for the general public, like the Chumash Casino does, and they open their books to show the public the annual economic impact their casino's have on the local economy (Note: The Chumash Casino's local impact was estimated at 150 million dollars in 2003), they might eventually win public support.

Any business that provides hundreds of jobs for surrounding communities, generates millions of dollars in payroll, state, and local taxes, uses local vendors, and contractors, and puts millions of dollars back into the communities would be considered a success by most business standards, but when it comes to Indian Gaming, the final judgment is still out in the eyes of many Americans.

Perchance A Wizard

By Reggie B. Cornejo

Published in 1982 in Orpheus

To dream a mystic hour,
The Long and somber kind,
It's where I get my power
That helps my magic mind.

I live the life of sorcerer;
I dwell in ageless time;
But Randi gives the sorcerer
The power for a rhyme;

There is no stronger wizard;
I conjure up the Black;
Perchance I am a lizard
Or the widow dressed in Black;

You wear a flower, a daffodil;
I kiss your lovely face;
Am I the golden daffodil
Or the wind upon your face?

(Note: The poem was published in California State University
Bakersfield's annual literary magazine in The magazine includes
short essays and poems written by professors, and former and current
students. I was honored to be picked as one of the contributors.)

The Vacation

By Reginaldo B Cornejo

(This short story was written one late night when I couldn't sleep. I couldn't sleep because I had taken a Semester off from college to save enough money to return to college the next semester, and I was worried I wouldn't return. To make sure I didn't lose my edge and study habits, I had decided to read as many books as I could while I was out of school. During this time, I decided to read books written by both Arthur Conan Doyle and Edgar Allen Poe, two of my muses that inspired me to become a writer. I guess I can say this story was influenced by both of these great writers. I never tried to sell the story because I felt it was written for my muses and not the general public. I hope my readers enjoy it.)

The Vacation

By Reginaldo B Cornejo

M Y LITTLE EXCURSION THAT WOULD soon become a nightmare started in the fall of 1972. I was living in the Los Angeles (also known as LA) area at the time, and as I drove out of my Los Angeles suburb that was close to down town LA, I found myself being impressed by the modern, although congested, beauty. I took in the splendor of the giant skyscrapers of down town Los Angeles and marveled at the growth and changes this area was still experiencing, in spite of the fact that more growth seemed impossible in this over crowded metropolis in Southern California.

As I headed out of town, I remembered I had to concentrate on the task at hand, which was an excursion south of the Border to Mexico. To be more exact, I was headed to a little town by the name of Guadalajara. Although I had never been in Mexico, or Guadalajara, I was headed to this town to visit a classmate/friend's grandparents to let them know that their grandchild, or my classmate, had recently passed away in an auto accident. The sad part of my trip was that my classmate's grandparents were Roger's only living adult relatives I knew of because Roger's parents had also died young. As I drove along, I told myself this trip was not going to be a fun trip, so I just needed to enjoy it as much as I could and get what I could out of it. Since Los Angeles is not too far from the Mexican border, I soon found myself on the Mexican side of the American/Mexican border going through customs, and where a well-timed under the table tip got me on my way.

As I drove away from the border and headed into Mexico, I found myself shocked to see the contrast between the American country side and Mexican country side. The transformation from well groomed and smooth paved freeways on the American side soon gave way to narrow and suspect highways that in America would be considered back roads, or two lane country roads. Although I felt a little uncomfortable, I soon found myself enjoying the drive because of the lush and virgin vegetation that was found on both sides of the road that I was driving on to my destination. I soon found myself thinking that a man could get lost in this vegetation if he got off the main road that I was driving on at the time. This area seemed to have the feeling that time had stood still in this ancient land. Since I was in a hurry, I found myself driving throughout the day till it was getting dark. Not knowing the area, I decided that it was time to stop and so I finally stopped in a small town that looked safe and sort of modern.

After a restful sleep in a decent hotel/motel that I managed to find in the dark, I found that daylight came quickly the next day, so I got up early and decided to hit the road for my destination "unknown." I am happy to say that some good people I met in the small town did give me some great directions and informed me the next big city I would hit would be Mazatlan. They also told me this town would be a good sign I was headed the right way and that I was getting closer to finding the home of my deceased classmate's grandparents. As I drove along, I found myself hoping that I would reach my destination in a few days so I could keep the schedule I had planned for this trip. I do want to note that I found the roads to be pretty good so I moved along pretty smoothly. As I drove along, I would sometimes stop along the way to get some packaged food or bottled sodas for fear of getting sick in a foreign country. I had been warned to not drink the water or eat raw vegetables.

I finally reached Guadalajara at four o'clock in the morning. Since it was so early, I found a coffee shop and got a cup of coffee to wait till I could get some instructions on how to find my ex-classmate's grandparents. Although I had an address and some directions, I knew I needed help finding the old couple's home. As daylight arrived, I finally got some help and used the directions I had been given to find the house. Since I was not in a hurry to be the bearer of sad news, I waited around till I saw people coming in and out of the home. I finally got up enough courage and headed for the door. As I knocked on the door, I felt I was having and out-of-body experience because it seemed like it took for ever for someone to answer the door. When the door finally opened, I found myself looking in the face of a kind looking older women, who evidently was my ex-classmate's grandmother. The kind looking lady then asked if I was the gentleman who had called them from America about their grandson. I reluctantly said yes, and she asked me to come in and sit down. As she called out to the others in the house, I saw the home explode with lights and the room was soon filled more curious people.

The next day I found myself walking around with one of my ex-classmate's female cousins. She was mostly of Spaniard blood. The reason I noticed this fact was because of her big blue eyes and beautiful blonde hair. As we walked around the town, she showed me the dam her family had described in the two letters we wrote to each other. It was just as they had described the dam in their letters. After looking over the design and the structure of the dam, I found the dam to be just what I wanted to see when I arrived in this town. Since I was majoring in Engineering at the University of California in Los Angeles, or UCLA, the "old school" design of the dam was one of the main reasons I had decided to make the long drive into this city in Mexico, and the curiosity of my minor studies in investigative work and police science (that I hoped would help me dabble in part-time detective work) had also peaked my interest to come down into Mexico.

Having seen and found what I had hoped to find, my ex-classmate's cousin then decided to take me to her favorite restaurant in town and feed me. While we were eating, I learned that her name Sofia had been her great-grandmother's name. As Sofia and I had lunch, she informed me that her town's football team had a big winning tradition and that was the reason her town's football field, or soccer field, was one of the best in the Mexican states or provinces. While we were having lunch, I was lucky and met some of the locals. Although some of the young ladies were nice, I felt none of them compared to Sofia my guide. Sofia stood about five foot two had dark brown eyes, and had a face like an angel.

On the way to her house, I noticed this town had a very old church that had been built with the architectural design of the early 1800s so I asked her if we could go in and look around. Sofia smiled and said she would see if anyone was in the church so I could study the interior design and enjoy her hometown's place of worship. When we finally found someone and were allowed to enter the old church, I first noticed all of the church furnishings were very old and had been hand made and had probably been made over a hundred years ago too. I also noticed the carved designs on the walls of the church had been hand carved and chiseled by hand. Finally, I noticed the statues of the church were all hand carved and made of either wood or stone. The old saying "They don't make them like that anymore" quickly jumped into my head, and this thought reminded me of the fact that our modern world in America was mostly filled with machine made and computer designed things that couldn't match God's creations.

Sofia and I were walking and I was so enchanted with what I had just witnessed and inspected that I didn't speak or say a thing to her. As we walked I was suddenly surprised by a procession that appeared to be a funeral procession. I started to say something, and ask about what we were witnessing, but my young lady friend suddenly cut me off and silenced me. I didn't say a thing because I could tell she was very serious. As the procession passed and left us alone, I noticed that Sofia had lost that don't say a thing look on her face, so I asked her why she had silenced me completely during what I was sure was a simple funeral procession. "After all," I said to her, "It's only a funeral procession."

As the mourners and the deceased disappeared around a corner, Sofia looked at me and with a look that said, "Okay, now that the moment is over, I will explain, since you are an American, or foreigner." When she started explaining what we had just witnessed, she first informed me that what we had witnessed was no ordinary funeral. She explained the dead person in the horse-drawn hearse had not died of natural causes. She informed me she knew this fact because of the decorations that had been put all over the hearse to ward of evil. She could tell I was confused so she added, "The dead man in the hearse had been murdered or killed by an evil demon." I asked her how she knew all of these facts, and she then informed this man was one of many other locals who had died in their sleep in the middle of the night during the past ten months. Although these people had been in good health and had shown no signs of being sick, they had all suddenly died from what appeared to be starvation. The sad part of these deaths was that no local doctor could figure out the sudden cause of death of these once healthy people and why their bodies all looked gaunt and under nourished.

After she stopped speaking, I found myself at a loss for words because I didn't want my first words out of my mouth to sound like I was being a "know it all," or a smart mouth American citizen. When I finally spoke, I asked her why she felt these people had been murdered. She then pointed to the river that ran next to their city and that powered the big electric power plant that I had come to her city to study for my major. I followed Sofia to the river's bank and I noticed she had picked up a white flower that sort of looked like the lilies I had seen in America's flower shops. I told her the flower was pretty and that we had nothing like these flowers growing in our ponds or rivers. I then asked her what the flower, or flowers, had to do with the funeral and my question I had asked her. After a pause, Sofia asked me if I had noticed the coffin had these flowers on top of it instead of a wreath or carnations. I thought back and remembered she was right. I had noticed the small white flowers on the coffin. We finally arrived at her home and sat down to rest after our long walk. However, in my mind, I kept thinking back to the chain of events that included the funeral, the flowers, and finally the fact that Sofia had said the man in the coffin had been murdered by a demon, and he had not died of natural causes.

I woke up early the next day, and since it was Saturday and no body was going to work, I offered to take the family for a drive and pay for lunch somewhere in the city. Since the family was in mourning from the death of my ex-classmate, they decided to take me up on the offer so we all piled into my car. The grandfather seemed to be the one who enjoyed the ride and free lunch the most. I know I can come to this conclusion because as we drove around town the grandfather sat up and waved at of his friends he saw when we stopped either for traffic or to eat and shop. Since towns like the one I was visiting often had few cars, I noticed that some of the locals often asked Sofia and her grandparents if I was a rich man. When they would learn I was just a college student, they would laugh and couldn't believe it.

After our drive and lunch, I got bold and asked Sofia's semi-grandparents if I could have Sofia show me more of their town. Since Sofia was still quite young, and under the care of Roger's grandparents, I found myself practically begging Sofia's grandparents to allow Sofia to show me more of their town. During our drive, I noticed that a house we had passed had the same small white flowers on the door of the house. Before we went too far, I backed up the car and asked Sofia why this house had the same flowers as the ones on the casket we had seen at the funeral. As I looked at Sofia's face for an answer, her face got pale white and she said, the demon had probably struck again over night and the people in the house were trying to save the person that had been attacked. As for the flowers, she added the flowers served to keep away the demon these people called the "Lechusa." She then added a Lechusa was a mythological creature that according to legend sucked the soul and blood out of the person or victim it decided to attack. Since the attacks would occur over several days, the flowers were an attempt to keep the demon out of the house.

Instead of just accepting Sofia's information and driving off, I found myself feeling the need to go into the house and learn more about this so

56

called creature called a Lechusa. As we walked towards the front door of the house, I felt lucky to find that Sofia knew so much about this creature, or demon, that evidently was terrorizing this small city. After some discussion at the front door of the house with the flowers, Sofia and I were allowed to go into the home with the flowers on the door. It was dark in the home, and although the home had electricity and lights in the home, I noticed the occupants only had an oil lamp on to light the inside of the home.

Since I was trying to get all of the information I could get on this mythological creature these people felt was the cause of their grief and deaths, I decided to try to get as much information on this creature from Sofia. I guess I can say the curiosity from my studies in police science and investigations from my minor had kicked in and I found myself wanting to play detective like Sir Arthur Conan Doyle's great detective Sherlock Holmes. I decided to start to get as much information on this creature by collecting as much information and facts as I could about how this creature allegedly worked and killed. The people noticed I was very methodical in my investigative techniques so when I asked to be allowed to get close to the person that had been allegedly attacked the night before, they agreed. The first thing I noticed about the victim was that he had a high fever. Since the victim had a high fever, I also noticed he was sweating a lot, was very weak, and when he coughed, he would cough up very little fluids. Since I had studied about third world deceases like malaria in my world history courses, I told myself the man could be suffering from something as simple as malaria.

Not wanting to insult the local doctor who might have already visited and treated this sick man, I didn't say anything to the family members. But, since my curiosity had been peaked, I asked if I could turn the man over on his side because he appeared to be choking or having stomach cramps that made him curl up in a fetal position. As the man turned, I noticed a dark looking spot, or what appeared to be a big purple bruise on his hip area. Having been a athlete most of my life, as I looked closer at what I thought was a bruise, I found myself saying to myself that this was not your run of the mill bruise. Although I knew I was probably breaking their tradition of only having a lamp, I quickly begged them to turn on their electric light so I could get a better look at the alleged bruise. As I inspected the bruise closer, I found myself thinking that what I was looking at was not a bruise but some kind of bite or "leach like" open wound. Under the lights, I noticed the open wound had a round row of tiny needle like punctures or holes, and that these punctures were seeping fluid and blood, like an over sized mosquito bite.

When I finished my study of the wound and decided I had seen enough, I turned to Sofia and asked her if these kinds of wounds were common on the victims of this creature called the Lechusa. She said since the families thought the victims were cursed or were dying from a decease they often did not touch them or take their clothes off once they were stricken. "According to Legend," said Sofia, "the reason the people or family members didn't touch the victims too much was because they were scared the demon would get mad at them and then select them as his next victim." Since Sofia had told me earlier that the doctor often couldn't do much for the victims, I then asked Sofia why the family members of the stricken victims didn't demand a more thorough study of the victim's body, and her answer surprised me when she said that most of the families in this city didn't often have the extra money for too many medical expenses so they usually didn't push the issue or ask for more information than they could afford.

As we talked, the victim on the bed started to move around and started to have what appeared to be some kind of shot of pain that was followed by a big coughing fit and the spitting up of blood. Since the family members were scared to touch him, not one of the members attempted to help so I quickly helped the man sit up in an upright position. This feeble attempt to ease the man's pain appeared to help him a little, but before I could do more, the man started having trouble breathing and died within minutes of the start of the initial pain. Poor Sofia was so shaken up that I noticed she had left while I was trying to help the man. Not being able to do much more for the grieving family, I covered their loved one's head with the sheet and followed Sofia outside. But then, I found I couldn't find her.

As I looked around for Sofia, I finally noticed that she had simply gone back to my car and was sitting in it. I slowly entered my car on the driver's side and looked at her and then I said, "I'm sorry that you had to see that bad bruise and the man's death." Having nothing else to say, I then started my car and drove Sofia home in complete silence. As she left the car, Sofia smiled and gave me a sisterly kiss on my cheek. I could only smile back and then I went for a drive to get some fresh air and a cup of coffee.

The next day I woke up early because I'd had a tough time staying a sleep, and the events of the previous day had created more questions than answers for me. As I sat at the table this early morning, I noticed Roger's grandfather had also gotten up early and was getting a cup of coffee from the fresh pot I had just made. He sat down and smiled, and then asked, "So why are you up so early, Jeff?" I smiled and told Grandpa, as he liked to be called, "I feel like I was sent here to help this town with this so called demon, or Lechusa. The problem is that I just don't know what I'm supposed to do for the people of this town." He slowly took a drink, and with a look that told me, "Don't worry young man; you'll figure it out," he said, "From the look on your face, I think you might be right, and I feel God sent you here to help us." We both smiled and then both took sips of our warm coffee, and in my heart, I felt he might be very right.

After I finished my coffee, I decided to ask Grandpa a few questions about this demon that evidently was terrorizing this town. I first asked Grandpa what he knew about this creature or fathom. As he sipped his coffee, Grandpa told me a short story about one of his friends who had allegedly been one of this demon's victims. He told me his friend had always been healthy and had seldom been sick, even though he had reached the age of 60s years old. This man was so strong that he had been the local butcher all of his life. His meat shop was one of the best in the area, and people would come from far away areas because his meat was always fresh and clean. One day, as he was walking past his friend's butcher shop, he noticed that it was not open and it was way past the time he always opened his shop. When he looked in the shop, he could tell his friend had not been in the shop. Knowing this was not right, he decided to go to the man's home; and when he knocked on the door, he found that his friend would not answer the door. Knowing something was wrong, Grandpa said he and the man's neighbor's decided to open a window and go inside to make sure the butcher was okay. When they finally found him, they found him on the floor next to his bed and you could tell he had struggled with something or someone.

As Grandpa continued his story, he then added that in the police report that was filed the police officers had stated that the man might have died at the hands of a burglar or thief. Since the man's death was considered a murder, the death of the man was eventually forgotten until about three months later when another person was found dead in their bed, and the circumstances were found to be almost the same, except in this case there had been very little struggle because the victim had been a woman. After the woman was found, about every month or two there would be a new victim. The problem was that although there usually was no sign of a struggle, the new victims were either dead or barely alive, and found too weak to revive. As for the age limit, the people that were being found dead or barely alive were usually age 55 or older. Since I had a strange feeling that Grandpa and the town's people knew there was a connection between these deaths and the demon, I decided to open up the topic by asking Grandpa if any of these victims had been found to have strange cuts or large bruises on their bodies. He smiled and said yes, but no one in the city wanted to admit to the large round like bruises that were common with all of the victims and the deaths.

I knew I was on the right track so I decided to ask Grandpa more questions about these victims that evidently had met their untimely ends in almost the same manner. I asked Grandpa if he could add a little more detail about the victim's bruises that I felt were more like open wounds that were some how connected to this demon the locals called a Lechusa. He then added that all of the victims had anywhere from one to three bruises on their bodies, and they were usually found either on the person's chest, leg, arm, or hip area. The other common thread I noticed came to me when Grandpa said that lately the victims had been older over 60s men and women, and that one of the male victims had been found to be holding bits of what appeared to be coarse fiber like hair, but it was not human hair. And one female victim that lived a few minutes after they found her had screamed, "dejame, dejame!" I asked Grandpa to translate for me, and he said it meant, "Leave me alone; leave me alone."

I was baffled and a little concerned because this creature's next victim could easily be Sofia's Grandpa or Grandmother. Since it was late summer, I asked Grandpa if everyone slept with their windows open. He said yes because this area was a tropical area and very warm at night. I then asked him if he could get the word out that for the next two nights could the town's people sleep with their windows closed, or just slightly ajar and locked. I also wanted the resident to make sure their doors were closed and locked tight. Although this idea worked for the two days, a few days later the alleged demon struck again. This time the demon or Lechusa had attacked a neighbor that lived right next door to Grandpa and Grandma.

When I arrived at the home of the latest victim, I found the lady in bed and breathing very shallow. The doctor had already been there and left, so I decided to do my own investigation by first checking the lady for any of the bruises I had seen on the other victim I had come in contact with a few days past. Although I tried to get some information from the lady through a translator, I had no luck because the lady, or victim, died before noon of that day. As I looked around the room, bed, and access areas, I found myself looking for any signs of forced entry or blood stains. I then decided to go out to my car and get the investigation kit one of my police science classes had asked us to buy for the course. My first instinct was to consider this death a murder and look for clues like finger prints. Unfortunately this act of investigative work turned up nothing. As I looked over the two windows in the room, I asked the neighbors who had discovered the lady if the windows had been open when they arrived. I got the answer that I expected when one of the neighbors said that the window I was standing next to had been open when she arrived. I then figured out that if this lady had been attacked by this so called demon it had entered through the window.

The next day I asked Grandpa to arrange a town-hall meeting later that evening. He informed me it was not necessary because since tomorrow was Sunday everyone would be at the local church for mass, and he would ask the minister if I could speak after the service. That Sunday I asked everyone to please keep their windows closed for their safety. This idea was good for about two weeks because from what I heard no victims were reported to the police or the church. Unfortunately, as they say, "the best laid plans of mice and men usually go awry," and in my case they did. After the two and a half weeks, I found myself facing a new attack. I had been in my room one early morning when Sofia burst into my room and told me her father had been attacked but had survived the struggle for his life. Sofia and I rushed to her parent's house to look for evidence, but by the time we got to the house, her mother had cleaned up the room, so if I could have found any new clues, they were now gone. I do have to say, that I did find one clue. I learned the alleged demon was very strong, very much alive, and not a spirit because it had ripped the window open.

A few days later, the demon, or Lechusa, attacked an older lady that lived by herself on a small hill that overlooked Sofia's city. Her window had also been ripped open and she had two big suction marks on her chest area. I finally got my finger prints that day, and to tell the truth, I felt someone had played a trick on us because the prints were nothing like what I expected, and they actually looked like a spider monkey's prints. I also found some hair caught on a splinter; it was like dog hair only finer. Now I knew I could try and trap this alleged demon, or what ever it was. I then asked Grandpa to get me some two-by-four planks to bar my windows with because I was going to leave my windows open to see if I could entice this demon to enter my room and attack me. I felt that if I could lure the demon into my room he wouldn't be able to escape after I closed the window.

As I lay in bed with my windows open, I felt a rush of adrenaline and also fear because I really didn't know how strong this creature was that was terrorizing this town and its occupants. I lay in bed for three nights waiting, and on the fourth night, I finally heard some noises near the open window. Since Sofia was worried, I reminded her that even if she heard a lot of loud noises coming from my room no one was to open the door. At about three in the morning, I finally heard what sounded like the flutter of bird wings and a pretty large shadowy figure appeared at my window and entered so softly that I barely heard it enter my room and land on my bed. I then felt it make its way close to me and my chest. Before it could get near my chest, I quickly grabbed for its body and pushed it off the bed. This quick move only stunned it for a minute because before I knew it the creature was back and trying to over power my resistance. When it noticed that I was a match for it in strength, the demon decided to fly out the window; but before the beast found the window, I ran over and closed it. It was now trapped. Although it was dark in my room, I could here it squealing like a giant mouse.

As I ran for the light switch, the door to my room opened; it was Sofia. I guess her nerves had gotten the best of her, and she had decided to help; however in her haste to help me, she had given the creature an opening to escape. The creature headed for the door and then it crashed through one of the glass windows in the next room and went out into the night. I felt I had missed my chance. I quickly ran after the beast and found the beast could fly silently like an owl and it could move about throughout the city without being noticed. As I watched it fly away, I told myself that it looked a lot like a big barn owl, which more than likely helped it move about un-detected. The only thing that gave it away was the fact that it had long appendages hanging down off of its body.

I decided to follow the demon in my car because I noticed it was heading for the dam. So, as I drove off, I told Sofia to let her father and the police know where I was going. I drove like a bat out of hell as I followed the flying beast. When I arrived at the dam, I noticed it had flown into one of the watch towers built into the hydro plant area of the dam. I looked back towards the city, and I could see Sofia, her father, Grandpa, and some other men coming towards the dam, so I decided to follow the demon into the tower. I felt that if I didn't follow it we would lose it and miss our chance of either killing this thing or capturing it for science. Before I followed the beast, I decided that discretion was a better choice than haste, so I opened the trunk of my car and pulled out the gun I had brought along with me for safety and a flashlight.

I slowly entered the tower through the only opening I could find, and I turned on my flashlight. It was damp, cool, and dark in the tower so I felt a little scared and anxious as I entered. Since I had forgotten to turn off the lights on my car, I noticed they were sort of working like spotlights that shined a little light on the tower and dam. My 38 Special felt cool in my hand because as I walked deeper into the tower it started to get cooler. I didn't notice, but Sofia and the men were getting closer to the dam as I slowly made my way into the deepest part of the tower. As I got deeper into the tower, I noticed there was a broken down door in my way, so I slowly pushed it out of the way and started to slowly walk up some steps I found behind the door. I could here the creature flying up the path of these steps so I knew I was headed in the right direction. After climbing for about five minutes, I noticed the spiral staircase I had just climbed was so rusted I was lucky it had held my weight.

I strained my ears to hear any sound that might let me know where the beast or demon might be hiding. As I walked up a few more stairs, I tried to not make any noise. My eyes strained to penetrate the darkness, but it was just too dark for my eyes or my flashlight. It also didn't help that I had to keep the flashlight shining down at my feet so I wouldn't trip or fall. As I moved up the stairs, I finally felt an opening to my left so I shined my light into the room and slowly started to enter. Just as I entered the room, I suddenly heard the beating of wings and felt something grab my arm and neck. It was the beast, and it was trying to push me out of an opening that had been built into the wide opening I had entered. The opening was part of the viewing platforms that was used to inspect the dam in the daylight, but in the dark, it was a dangerous forty foot drop into a small ravine that was part of the dam's flood gates that was used to let water out when the dam got too full.

I found myself in a life and death struggle with the beast, so I decided to just get it over with and shoot the beast and let science be damned, but as I turned to shoot, I lost my gun somewhere in the dark. I swung at the beast and beat it with my fist but it was just too strong for me. I then decided to make a run for it and head back down the stairs; but! I found the beast was right behind me. I then decided to stay in the tower and see if Sofia and the men had arrived yet. I looked out the opening and yelled for help to the men coming towards the dam. I could see the men running towards me and entering the dam, so I knew that my best chance was to just keep fighting off the beast and survive. As I turned my head away from the opening I had used to yell for help, I suddenly felt a sharp pain on the back of my head. The creature had decided to forget pushing me out the opening and decided that it was kill or be killed. As I turned to push it away from my face and head, I finally got a good look at my tormentor and learned that this beast looked like something out of a person's nightmare or the "Twilight Zone."

The creature's features reminded me of a cross between an owl and a mosquito from the dinosaur era. Though it had no front or back feet or arms, it did have six thin like arms that allowed it to land quietly. Its body was also thin and mosquito like in design because it was sleek and slender. As for its wings, they were attached towards the center part of his back like today's modern dragonflies. The hideous part of this strange and ancient looking animal was its head which appeared to be a combination between a human head and that of an insect and it had no nose just small holes near its mouth opening that looked a lot like the mouth of today's giant leeches.

As I wrestled with the demon, I found it was too quick for me, and it soon had almost overpowered me again and was trying to knock me out. Just as it was about to strike a fatal blow to my head, I heard the sound of several shots being fired. The creature released its grip, and I then noticed we were both covered with blood. Since I could see the creature was badly injured, I then watched it as it headed for the big opening out of the tower. It stopped to look back and then it attempted to fly away, but it instead started dropping down towards one of the large power plant water way openings that were spewing out thousands of gallons of water. These openings were turning the electric turbines that produced the electricity for the town. As I watched it struggle to survive, I saw it struggle and then slowly sink into the depths of the dark rushing water.

As the men rushed towards me, I could tell Sofia's father had been one of the men who had fired the fatal shots that had killed the town's alleged demon. Sofia came up to me saw the blood and almost fainted, but I told her not to worry because none of it was my blood. As the men, Sofia, and I walked away from the dam, I looked back and felt some sorrow for the beast that evidently had found itself in the year 1972 of the modern day 20th Century and had simply been trying to survive the only way it knew how to do it. I also thought about the old movies and tales of Count Dracula and the flying bat that killed men and women to stay alive by drinking their blood. But when I looked at the creature through scientific eyes, I wondered if this creature was just a poor left over beast from the era of dinosaurs that once roamed earth's surface, when they ruled the earth.

The Miracle

By Reginaldo Cornejo

The Wizard often wonders

How life gets Complicated;

He sits intently and ponders

Was too much anticipated?

Was it only magic or

Only living schemes?

Life's a conjured miracle;

It tends to complicate.

Life's a flowered Musical

That's born to replicate...

(This poem was written while I was studying for a Social Psychology test in our college library in 1982. It just came to me, so I stopped studying and wrote it in about five minutes.)

News from Indian Country

Chumash Indians Offended by Ventura Newspaper Ad

By Reg. B Two Stones

(This news article was published in "The Native" magazine in the 1994 August issue. The magazine was published in Northern California to educate and inform Native Americans living on the west coast. I had the pleasure of writing for the magazine for over four years, till it moved to Arizona. I hope this article helps America's citizens see that although today's politically correct era appears to be in the business of protecting both the legal and illegal public living in America, it does not appear to include America's Native Americans and their culture.)

Native Magazine

News from Indian Country

Chumash Indians Offended by
Ventura Newspaper Ad

By Reg. B Two Stones

THERE MUST BE SOMETHING IN the air that makes everything look so clean and clear in Ventura. Maybe it's the ocean air itself or the light mist that settles in every evening after sunset. Or! Just maybe, it's the fact that long before there was the city of San Buenaventura, or the county of Ventura, there was the village of Shisholop—Chumash for "in the mud"—and its Native American population who lived in harmony with nature and the Great Spirit.

These Native Americans paddled their canoes between the village of Shisholop and other villages along the California coast and along the local Channel Islands. They traded fish, acorns, and other goods made by the craftspeople of other islands. They lived and played in what today is known as Ventura County.

Although the contributions of these Native Americans can still be found throughout Ventura and Ventura County, it appears their influence is losing its luster—a loss easily measured by an "ugly" ad published on June 16, 1994 in the Ojai Valley Voice, a local paper that is published in the area by a small city near Ventura, California.

The aforementioned "ugly" ad ran on page 14 of the Valley Voice, and it was a large 5 by 5 inch blocked ad with the words **UGH-INJUNS** in big bold print across the top of the ad. A nice drawing of an "INJUN" tee-pee was also found in the ad. Unfortunately, the ad had little to do with Native Americans and nothing to do with cultural sensitivity. The ad was instead pushing a surplus store in Ojai, California.

Letakots-Lesa (Eagle Chief) of the Pawnee once warned, "All things in the world are two. In our minds we are two—good and evil. With our eyes we see two things—things that are fair and things that are ugly... We have the right hand that strikes and makes evil, and the left hand full of kindness, near the heart. One foot may lead us to an evil way the other foot may lead us to good. So are all things two, and all two." Unfortunately, the publishers of this ad did not hear this warning because the ad was not taken as a joke by the local Native American population, including myself. They instead considered it "ugly" and insensitive to their culture.

When the issue of cultural sensitivity was brought to the attention of the Ojai Valley Voice, the newspaper's publisher, Jeff San Marchi, said he had warned the store owner of the "potential problems it could cause." San Marchi added that, "She (owner Joy Grove) told me to do it anyway." He concluded his statement by saying he had a bad feeling about the ad from the beginning.

When Grove was contacted at her business, she stated that she had discussed the potential sensitiveness of the ad, but had decided it wouldn't offend anyone. When it was explained to her that the ad painted a negative stereotype of Native Americans, she added, "I really am sorry. I guess it really was done in poor taste."

Publisher San Marchi also said the ad in question had not been published correctly. He added that part of the print had fallen off during production. "It was also supposed to say, "Heap Big Bargains, Little Wumpum." Perhaps San Marchi hoped to imply the ad was meant to be funny or a joke.

However, when we make light of another cultural, I hate to say it, but it is never funny.

In these times of growing accusations of racism and cultural clashes in both our courts and streets of America, I sense that too many Americans take it for granted that people do these things to be vicious and mean spirited. Yet from my article, I feel the facts found in this story show a lack of cultural understanding was the real problem and not viciousness. It appears to me that more people need to attend more Pow-Wows and read more stories about Native Americans by writers who understand the American Indian cultural so that a bridge of understanding can be created between Americans and Native Americans. This article attempts to do no more and no less. I wrote this article to heal the pain and to educate, not to accuse and create more tensions. Ah-Ho.

Shakespeare and Life

By Reggie Cornejo

To Shakespeare, a man so rare,

You made me learn of life;

When I was young, I slept on air,

Then I read your words,

And knew and learned of life;

My heart matured and grew its share;

The world was opened with your knife.

Sweet tender things grew harsh and bare.

Your words gave mine their sweet life.

(This poem was written after I read my first play by William
Shakespeare. My mother found a small book that had the title of
"The Complete Works of William Shakespeare," so she bought it
for me. I found myself reading the book day and night in school
(grammar school) and when ever I had time after school. As my
readers can see, this man's works started my fire to write.)

The Hispanic Outlook in Higher Education

Perspective

Teaching Shakespeare, Reaching Students

The Human Frailty Connection

By Reginaldo Cornejo

(I wrote this essay when I returned from teaching English in Japan. I had used some dialogue from some of Shakespeare's plays to get my student speaking English that was not part of a question and answer simple lesson plan. Since the students were used to the "Where is the train station? The train station is over there," question and answer lesson plans, I decided to get them out of their comfort zones by allowing them to read dialogue from Shakespeare's plays, and force them out of their comfort zone. When I returned to America to teach, I decided to use the human factor of my American students to show them the connection between their lives and William Shakespeare's characters. After I wrote this essay in 2/2001, I learned that Dr. Solomon O. Iyasere had written a paper on this idea or topic, so I added some of his findings to my essay. After all, his theory and ideas had been published before I decided to write about my simple Shakespeare lesson plans in Japan.)

So my short article I had written on my use of Shakespeare's works to help my Japanese Students would pop, I decided to create a very special cover photo to introduce my article. I decided to use it in my book too because I feel this article allows me to also honor a great college professor that I was honored to know and meet during my studies at Cal State University, Bakersfield.

The Hispanic Outlook in Higher Education

Perspectives

Teaching Shakespeare, Reaching Students

The Human Frailty Connection

By Reginaldo Cornejo

(Published February 12, 2001 in <u>The Hispanic Outlook in Higher Education</u>. I wrote this article because I wanted to help my students get more out of their education. This article is being published in my book with the gracious permission of the Hispanic Outlook. I wish to thank Suzanne Isa-Lopez for her kindness and professionalism.)

BE HONEST, WHEN WAS THE last time you thought to yourself: "Yes, I get to teach Shakespeare to my Hispanic/minority students." If you're an English Professor who has paid his or her dues, and you're smart enough to know that preparing a lesson plan is a necessity rather than a luxury, it might be time to consider your Hispanic/minority student's ethnic backgrounds when you present Shakespeare's plays, rather than just deciding "Shall I teach a tragedy or a comedy this week?"

In general, minority students (and most any students) tend to find Shakespeare boring, too hard, and dare I say it, a waste of time because "Those stories are so old. What do they have to do with me in the 21st Century?" This question causes some of us teachers to stumble, but there is an answer, to wit: "Although Shakespeare's characters are often depicted in the plays as larger than life, or colossuses, eventually they are presented as human beings with human frailties just like 21st Century people."

The bit of knowledge I present in the last paragraph is very important because it is a good starting point for any class dialogue. Take for example, Stanley Well's discussion of Caesar's greatness and pending doom as he enters Rome in Shakespeare's play Julius Caesar: "Shakespeare allows Caesar his full measure of worldly greatness. [But,] he also lets us see that the world-conqueror will before long, and sooner than he may expect, be 'barreled up in a brazen urn no bigger than a bowl...' (Shakespeare, A Life in Drama, 193-194). [As for] Caesar's vulnerability, [it] is implicit in what he says about himself: 'I rather tell thee what is to be feared. Than what I fear, for always, I am Caesar. Come on my right hand, for this ear is deaf...'" (193-194).

Turning to another human weakness, it goes without saying that "In Shakespeare's England, the existence of a pervasive tradition of color prejudice...has been convincingly documented by historians and literary scholars...Also well documented is the presence of overt racist attitudes— the impulse to regard black men in set negative ways in Shakespeare's Othello," says Dr. Solomon O. Iyasere (Teaching Shakespeare Othello to a Group of Multi-Racial Students, California English/Fall 1994, 8).

Why make this observation and approach this sensitive topic? Well, for one thing, many Hispanic and minority students deal with racial stereotyping in the 21st Century. This fact was recently documented in the Los Angeles Times' "Metro" section by Al Martinez, whose piece "The Frito Bandito Syndrome," discusses the continued use of minority stereotyping (June 4, 2000), and Debra Dickerson's "Opinion" piece, "Racial Profiling: Are We All Equal in the Eyes of the Law (July 16, 2000?" This piece addresses racial profiling by America's police departments when deciding which cars to stop for possible drug violations.

"You must read the play to learn more about yourself, about what others think of people who are like you, both 500 years ago and today." Dr. Solomon O. Iyasere

Although Shakespeare's Othello does not take on either of the aforementioned newspaper topics, it does deal with the contemporary problem that won't go away and what Dr. Iyasere notes is to this day a topic of a sensitive nature, "Interracial marriage and the difficulties of racism and interracial relationships (8)." "The fact is, adds Iyasere, 'although interracial marriages are no longer illegal, as Davidson points out, The marriage of a middle-age black man and a young white girl must, then and now, touch sensitive nerves in Black and White (8)." Since this issue remains sensitive in the 21st Century, we again see the connection between the past and present, and find a great place to start a discussion. (Note: This was not in my original essay; but, I am married to a white female, and my wife and I have on occasion suffered the sting of racial prejudice from both minorities and whites during our marriage and that is why I feel this fact is a great starting point for a discussion on profiling.)

By now many instructors reading this essay are thinking, "Why use this vehicle to discuss these plays?" Well, since minority students must deal with all these volatile topics on a daily basis, why not give them a chance to voice their opinions on them and apply their opinions to Shakespeare's plays. "Paradoxically, says Dr. Iyasere, "the existence of racial problems in Othello…affects our idea of Othello and makes a difference to the action and catastrophe…the absence or presence of racist attitude inevitably determines one's response to Othello." After making this observation, Iyasere continued by adding, "To avoid teaching the play because of the emotionally charged, sensitive nature of its subject is to deny students the opportunity of experiencing one of Shakespeare's most memorable tragedies and of confronting, through the play, the difficulties of racism and interracial relationships which continue to trouble us today (8)."

Given that many minority students carry their own responses to race, which might have been conceived through some personal experience, the instructor must walk a fine line when presenting Shakespeare via this approach. A student's negative or positive experience could, as Dr Iyasere says, "[arouse] their own latent prejudices, which would then interfere with their emotional and intellectual apprehension for the play." Yet, I feel this problem can be avoided if we instructors remember the introductory premise that Shakespeare's characters and topics are still contemporary because they are presented as human beings with human frailties. Approaching these works in this manner helps us teach our students to deal with their own experiences and social prejudices in a nurturing and scholastic atmosphere, and allows them to vent in a non-threatening situation.

As Instructors, our job is to help our students learn to pose academic questions, find answers through organized research methods, and communicate in a professional manner so they can learn to function in society. If we instructors accept this statement, then why not present Shakespeare in a context of contemporary issues, which gives students a chance to sharpen these skills, master Shakespeare's great plays, and deal with their personal prejudices. Scary as this idea might seem, isn't it worth the challenge to help them learn to understand the greatness of Shakespeare and, as Dr Iyasere says, "see what is there, in the plays, as distinct from merely seeing a narcissistic mirror of their own experiences and social prejudices (8)?"

I know my fellow teachers might ask, "How can I be sure that my students won't lose their focus when they discuss hot topics that might causes anger or degrade their existence?" The answer, from my experience, is not an easy one, but believe me, there is an answer. It comes in the form of accepting that Shakespeare deals with real human emotions and frailties in his plays. And by dealing with the provocative issues in the plays of racism, stereotyping, interracial marriages, and personal weaknesses, you help your students evaluate "the characters and situations in terms of personal situations and private values" (Iyasere 10).

By presenting Shakespeare in this format, you allow literature to function as part of the student's existence, a key point, since "...literature," says Iyasere, "is written to affect those who write and read it (10)." This said, I now come to my final and most important premise. We teachers have to believe that our personal emotions and experiences are very necessary and relevant to the study of Shakespeare because as Dr. Iyasere adds, "If a work of art cannot speak directly to our experiences or present interests, it can offer us little insight into human nature" (10).

The formula for presenting Shakespeare in this format is not set in stone, but I believe that any experienced instructor will find a way to approach each play so that the students are allowed to feel the human elements (be they racial, religious, or sexual) found in the plot. To those teachers who feel that they need a little more help with methodology, I respectively offer Dr. Iyasere's warning that you go about it "slowly, step by step, honestly, and openly" (10). And the next time your students ask why they have to read Shakespeare, you might answer them with what I believe is a good answer that applies to students of all colors and genders. Although I have my own answer, I am going to yield to Dr. Iyasere because I feel his answer predates my own prejudice or reason. According to Dr. Iyasere, his answer was given when one of his black students asked him, "Why should I read Othello?" Dr. Iyasere replied, "I would say, you must read the play to learn more about yourself, about what others think of people who are like you, both 500 years ago and today" (9).

Solitude

By Reginaldo Cornejo

White!
A dream at night
That's lost in love;
The Glow of Light
Soft like a dove;

Soft!
I live the life,
And hold your hand;
Cuts like a knife,
Yet! It's lost in sand;

Night!
We are the one;
The life is true;
You breathe for none;
Is there a clue?

(I wrote this poem while waiting for the results of my Master's exit exam that I had to take to earn my MA in English Composition. The test was a six-and-a-half hour closed book test and I had to quote verbatim from 60 authors and 30 critics and earn a B or better. I passed but felt like my achievement had been tainted, cheapened, and my pride taken from me to earn my MA.)

A member of a tribe sets up his tippy at one of the many Pow-Wows that are often held on California University properties. This PNACI's tippy was set up at California State University, Bakersfield's campus during a two day celebration of life for many local Native Americans.

The Native

Our People—Our Pathways

Call Me PNACI

By Reg. Barroso Two Stones

(This article or news story was published in February of 1994 in <u>The Native</u> magazine. I decided to write this piece after I attended a Pow-Wow in the Winter. Although I had thoroughly enjoyed myself at the Pow-Wow, I found myself thinking about the discussion I had with Wolfhawk Martinez, a Yaqui and Comache Elder I met at this Pow-Wow. Although this story is from the 1990s, I feel it still rings true in 2019.)

The Native

Our People Our Pathways

Call Me PNACI

By Reg. Barroso Two Stones

W HAT DOES PNACI STAND FOR? That is to say, what does this word
mean to Native Americans? Could it stand for a new tribe, singing
group, Native American food, song title, or a group of indigenous people?
According to Wolfhawk Martinez, a Yaqui/Comanche elder, PNACI stands
for all the above and much more, especially pride.

The pride Wolfhawk is talking about in the last paragraph is what
prompted this Torrance, California elder to send his definition to newspapers
in 32 American states and to 53 newspapers throughout the world, and to
attend Pow-Wows throughout California to spread his word. Columbia,
Germany, Japan, Australia, Belgium, and Finland were just a few of the many
countries Martinez contacted to spread his message.

In the words of Wolfhawk Martinez, "To get the full intended message
of these five letters, we must understand that PNACI (Pen-ah-cee) is a "very
old word that means anyone who is descended of the old ones that were
indigenous to the Western Hemisphere." Martinez added that the word
PNACI survived because "a small number of elders and medicine people
who lived in the Southwestern United States and in remote regions of the
Sierra Madres of northern Mexico still use this word."

So, is the word PNACI so important to Native Americans that Wolfhawk
Martinez must devote his own time and money to spread its definition?
According to Wolfhawk Martinez, the answer is yes because it allows us to
"preserve our race and sustain our culture so that we may again be the true
role models in the preservation of mother earth."

"I merely offer a very old word preserved with dignity by the Elders of
our race that is based on 'truth and facts,'" said Wolfhawk Martinez. "It's (the
word PNACI) an alternative to calling oneself Indian, Indio, or American
Indian," added Wolfhawk.

Martinez's last statement is in keeping with his opinion that the word "Indian" is connected to the genocide of the Native American tribes which began or started the day Columbus set foot on Native American soil and called the indigenous of America "Los Indios," or "the Indians."

Wolfhawk Martinez and his people, like most Native Americans, feel that when Native Americans allow themselves to be called Indian, they are condoning the grievous actions and misdeeds for which Columbus and all the Europeans who followed stood for and in many ways championed. "We offer a chance to choose," added Martinez with a gleam in his eyes. "Allowing people to choose has always been the way of our people. We allow individuals to choose for themselves without the fear of being chastised by others for their choice," concluded Martinez.

When Wolfhawk was asked if his campaign was going well, he responded by producing several letters from various organizations that had responded favorably. The National Geographic Society (NGS) was among those groups that had responded positively. According to Wolfhawk, Patrick J. McGeehan of the NGS had written, "We appreciate the benefit of your views on the matter. Your letter is circulating among senior staff members. Thank you for writing."

With the growing influx of migrants entering America from India—people who refer to themselves as Indians—Martinez's argument for a new word to identify America's indigenous Native Americans may find a place in history yet!

(Note: Although I am sure Wolfhawk Martinez and his tribe pushed hard for this change, I am sad to say that I never heard from Indian Country, or the Native American "Red Road," that this word had caught on in use among America's Tribes.)

Calm's Satire

By Reginaldo B Cornejo

The Secret
Of the
Sunshine is
Hidden in
Our prayers.

The power
Of His
Glory is
What happens
In our hearts.

(This poem is among my earliest attempts to express myself in poetry. Although the poem is short, truncated, and simple, I feel like the Japanese Haiku poems that it speaks volumes.)

This building is found on the campus of Shibaura Institute of Technology. The classroom I used to teach my TESL/TEFL classes was on the second floor. The building also served as the place to hold my "free talk" lessons. In some ways it was my home away from home till my contract ended.

Attitudinal Changes of an American Minority Instructor:

A Look Back at Japan

By Reg B Two Stones Cornejo

(Note: I wrote this story after I completed my second full-time teaching contract in the Kanto Region of Japan. I had intended to send it to a new magazine that I had learned of during my second time in Japan. I had met the senior editor in Japan, and he encouraged me to send in a story. To make a long story short, during the time I was writing and completing this article, I was offered a full-time job working for America's Federal Government so I never sent the story in to be published. I now offer it to my readers in my latest book. I hope you enjoy it and learn a little more about Japan.)

Attitudinal Changes of an American Minority Instructor:

A Look Back at Japan

By Reg. B Two Stones Cornejo

E VERY FALL, AS TEACHERS, WE return to the classrooms and accept new teaching assignments or positions in new cities, states, or countries. Being professionals, we arrive at these new jobs or job sites with preconceived notions about how good, or bad, these new jobs or assignments will be, and with a lot of apprehensions as we prepare for any worst case scenarios, just in case it happens. This was the mind set I had when I arrived at my new teaching position I had accepted in Japan for the second time. Although I had been in Japan before and taught for this company (or school) before, I really didn't know what to expect this time around. The contract I had accepted was a short one that would have me working for a company called Westgate Corporation. I was to teach English as a Foreign Language at Shibaura Institute of Technology (SIT) in a city named Higashi-Omiya in Japan, again.

As I walked off the plane at Japan's Narita International Airport, I kept telling myself I had decided to accept this contract because I had not been given a choice by the California Junior College English Department heads. After all, I now knew they just weren't going to hire a minority English College professor on a full-time basis, or as a tenured JC professor. Yes, I often found part-time work with these colleges in the spring semesters, but these jobs just weren't paying the bills. Besides I told myself, I am going to teach in another country again, and for some people, this opportunity is a life time dream. "Think about it," I told myself, "You get to see new places, visit areas of Japan that you dreamed of when you were young, no research papers to grade in transfer level English classes, and new fresh faces and people to meet. This kind of change is the perfect escape from everyday life and everyday routine lesson plans."

But, if I was so apprehensive about taking this job in Japan, why had I come to this decision, or conclusion? In a word, despair was my demon: You see, last fall, after sending out well-over ninety applications for fulltime (and some fulltime (and full time/part-time) tenure track positions throughout California, my inability to secure a teaching contract, or an interview, at any junior college had finally wore me down. These results had made me desperate because I had my college school loans to pay, and the bills were piling up. Truth be told, I was ready to quit teaching and return to journalism and become a reporter again. To make matters worse, I was becoming a mental and physical mess as the author of the book Going to Pieces Without Falling Apart describes in his book.

So, in the interest of personal growth, sanity, and survival, I decided to accept another job contract with a great company that I had worked for before that was, as I said, called Westgate Corporation of Japan. The school I would be teaching at, again, would be my old haunt Shibaura Institute of Technology that is located in the quaint city of Higashi-Omiya, Japan. This college campus can be reached via the Utsunomiya Japanese train line. Since I had taught at this school before, I knew that Shibaura was a co-educational campus that served some 3,240 students (stats from 1999-2003) who were mostly engineering majors. Although the college is very modern, to me, the fact that Shibaura's students were a group of classy young men and young women, and Shibaura's staff members were top grade, is the reason I had accepted to teach at this college again. The other reason I accepted to teach and live in this area again is that Shibaura is located in the Saitama Prefecture (like our counties in the US) which is mostly a rural setting.

I want to add that I also liked the fact that Shibaura and my future home would be located about an hour from both Shinjuku and Ikebukuro, which are two of my favorite night life cities. Some of the other attractions that made my mind up to teach in this area again included the fact that I was also close to Tokyo, two great parks, and the famous Rainbow Bridge that in many ways rivals San Francisco's Golden Gate Bridge in design and appearance. I do want to add here that this area does get pretty humid during the summer months because of the rains and heat.

So, why do I like the Saitama Prefecture? Well, Saitama is a great place to experience Japan's old and new culture. This area is also home to many tourist attractions that include the Bonsaimura. I want to note the Bonsaimura is a village that is devoted to growing world famous bonsai trees. Saitama also offers the Saitama Prefectural Museum of Natural History and the annual Chichibu Festival that offers fireworks and floats to celebrate the festival that comes in December every year. While these attractions were more than enough to attract me to return to Saitama, I am happy to say that these events and attractions attract millions of tourists from all over the world every year. I guess you could say this California State University, Bakersfield graduate and professor that was born on the wrong side of the tracks was courted and won over by this Japanese Prefecture.

As for what attracted me to return to Shibaura Institute of Technology (SIT) four years later (2003) to teach their students, I have to confess that Shibaura's small college atmosphere, that is big enough to provide its students a solid education in Engineering, was a big factor. I guess you could say the college has a quaint small college atmosphere and it really is not that small. But even more important to me, from the first day I arrived at this college back in 1999, I felt at home. Don't ask me to explain; I don't think I could in a million years. I did find that it had the same feeling as California State University, Bakersfield, which is the school I graduated from with my Masters in English.

I want to add that by American standards Shibaura's buildings are very modern in design. The school consists of about 10 main buildings that include modern classrooms, science labs, a very nice library, a student union with computer rooms, a theater (that I had the honor of doing a voice over for one of the plays that was performed by some of my students), practice rooms for music majors, a book store, your typical administrative offices, and a very clean cafeteria that the students use daily. I did try some of the Japanese dishes of the cafeteria, and I have to say the food was very good. I had the pleasure of trying some of the Japanese dishes and one day they served Italian food. By the way, if the staff or students ever need a junk food fix, the school's bookstore is happy to provide these types of snacks for their convenience.

Another feature I enjoyed about SIT that sent me back to teach at this school was the campus itself. I found the grounds and buildings to be very tidy and groomed. Thanks to the school's staff of male and female landscapers/ groundskeepers, the school's grounds were kept expertly manicured. These hard working people could be seen working on campus from sun up to sun down. Since I was a guest on this school's campus, I always felt a need to address and greet these hard working people who toiled diligently and to my surprise always took the time to say Ohayo, or "good morning," to me and the rest of the staff at this school. Although I was a "gaijin" (foreigner), I was never left out of the traditional, but melodic, "ohayo gozaimasu sensai," which is a very formal way of saying "good morning professor" in Japanese. To a Hispanic/Native American educator who had just left a country whose college education system had just rejected him as an employee or tenured college professor, this warm welcome, or greeting of respect, was like being allowed to find Nirvana. I mean think about it I told myself, I am getting a chance to teach Japan's future leaders; so, I guess I could say this job was exactly what I needed to raise my spirits and cure my sagging career and ego.

And if there was anyone who ever needed a career boost, it was me; I have to say that at this time in my life I really needed an ego boost and a chance to use my education and teaching skills. I also enjoyed the fact that I was getting more teaching experience. After all, this job was at one of Japan's better Engineering Universities and was not some part time K-12 substitute teacher's job in California; this job, I told myself, was a chance to learn new methodologies, try new lesson plans, create new teaching tools; most important of all, I had a chance to use Japanese curriculum and methodologies at a major Japanese university setting with Japanese students.

Looking back, I would now describe my Japanese Students as a mix of quiet and reserved traditional students and some very outgoing personable and westernized students: For those readers not familiar with Japan, traditional Japanese male students wear 50/50 material dress shirts (some T-shirts), jeans/slacks, and casual shoes or sneakers. Their female counterparts usually wear conservative skirts, slacks, loose jeans, blouses or loose fitting T-shirts, sweaters, blazers, pumps, sneakers, and are very quiet shy young ladies in school. Yes, these students do let their hair down when not on campus, but they do not go crazy.

To get an idea or image of the westernized Japanese students, all my readers have to do is to look around on any American college campus and you'll get the idea. Oh, before I move on, I want to add that most of my westernized Japanese students had their hair dyed either beach-boy or beach-girl blond, had blue or green contact lenses, and loved to watch the old re-runs of Beverly Hills 90210.

Although I enjoyed all of my students, the biggest reward I feel I received from my students was their respect and politeness concerning me and the rest of the college staff. Since I was obligated to hold office hours and "Free-talk," I was able to get to know my students' personalities both in class and after class. I should also note that "Free-talk time" consisted of one hour sessions that I held in an open forum where any student could come by and discuss their homework from my English class or chat about any topic that was on their mind in English. They could not use any Japanese while talking to me.

So which students studied harder of these two groups what curriculum or lesson plans worked best on these students? Well, I have to say the answer to each of these questions was quite surprising to this CSU Bakersfield system grad. At the end of the school term, I found that both my westernized and conservative students studied hard and took their TEFL/TESL English language course very seriously. They also took their other courses just as serious. Although the students' motivation for studying English varied, the major reason these students were taking my extra curriculum English class (and couldn't be overlooked) was their chances for future employment in Japan's tight and impacted job market.

During free talk time and sometimes over lunch, I learned that many of my students were looking for jobs with Japanese companies that had international ties and jobs overseas in English speaking countries like America, England, and Australia to name a few countries. And of course, to get these jobs in these countries, these Japanese students knew they would get the opportunity if they could speak English well. I also learned the ability to speak English was often the difference between getting a job in Japan, and not getting a career job. I also learned that some of students were learning English to be able to participate in overseas studies and/or travel to foreign countries for long stays.

As for the question of which curriculum and lesson plans worked best, I have to say that I had to make some attitude adjustments as the days passed by and I got to know my students better. Having taken courses to teach English as A Second Language and English as a Foreign Language and Linguistics during my graduate studies and having preconceived ideas, I found that some of my preconceived ideas didn't apply to any of these students from Japan. I also want to note I had come to Japan with the idea that the tools in Second Language Acquisition I had used in America could also be applied or used on my Japanese Students. But! I quickly learned this was, and was NOT the case. I found myself putting my preconceived notions aside as the days went by because the Company I signed on with had prepared and created lesson plans that they knew would work on these Japanese students. Since Westgate Corporation had been using their lesson plans and second language acquisition tools for many years, I found that this company had a finger on the pulse of their student's needs. One of my favorite tools was something called a "Daily Planner" tool that included many suggested lesson plans too. The "Daily Planner" also included objectives for the lessons and in many ways were much like the lesson plans I had used in America to teach transfer level, non-transfer level, and ESL/EFL English courses.

As the weeks passed by, I did notice one key concept or pattern in the lesson plans created by my employer. The lesson plans included very little "listening" or passive learning on the students' part. While the curriculum and recommended lesson plans stressed the audio-lingual approach and made me use an "Ask-Answer-Add speaking model that followed natural speech or conversations to force the students to speak English, I felt the one element that was missing from this approach was a recommended "silent" or "pre-speaking" period as proposed by Patricia Dunkel in her article: "listening in the Native and Second/Foreign Language: Toward an Integration of Research and Practice" (TESOL Quarterly, Volume 25, No. 3, Autumn 1991, P431-457).

I now want to explain that the Ask-Answer-add Production-oriented speaking model included four sentences that were used to create an English Conversation between two people; its basic components included an opening question, an answer, another question and an answer to the question that either could or could not be expanded upon by the students. And, although I found most of my students could parrot and repeat well in group unison during the choral drill phase, I often found or noticed the majority of my students could seldom create or add information or new sentences during their pairs work, and/or extend the conversation any more. This problem also appeared during periods when my students were asked to discuss topics given to them from English Flash Cards. These results lead me to believe that my students were suffering from a phenomenon that Patricia Dunkel labeled as "task overload" (Dunkel, 436).

According to Dunkel, "...task overload appears in learners who are required to speak at too early a stage in their second language acquisition. [It] inhibits language acquisition and the exercise and development of discriminatory skills: [It also] creates anxiety and encourages interference from L1 or [first language learners] (Dunkel, 436)." The results are usually language learners who can "vocalize" or "parrot," which according to Dunkel, does not have the same status as "speaking." So! The student or students are in reality "virtually incompetent in understanding the spoken language" and are not capable of creating original dialogue and sentences" (Dunkel, 436).

My students' inability to extend their conversations, I found, were a perfect example of Dunkel's phenomenon as she explained it. I therefore decided to add a "cognitive advantage" (short silent period) period to the lesson plans Westgate had created for me to use so it would allow my students a chance to delay oral exercises before they broke up into pairs for group work. The "silent period" was initiated after the choral practice, and it included a short ten minute lecture on the topic being discussed in the "Ask-Answer-Add" model (Note: I did this to add more background on the topic being discussed in the lesson plan.) and taking questions from advanced students who were willing to expose "their vulnerable language egos" in class (Dunkel, 436).

In fairness to my students, I want to add that I did tell my students I was adding a pre-discussion period (silent period) to the class to help them relax before they broke up into pairs. As the term went on, I was happy to notice many of my quiet/shy students started to speak more during their pairs work and flash card exercises. Most of my students who had displayed task overload symptoms started to open up more in my class, and I found they were willing to take more chances at the beginning of class by greeting me with a shy "Hello, good morning, or good afternoon." Their new found confidence, of course, made me happy for them.

Although I don't know if adding the "silent period" to my lesson plans helped all of my students improve their comprehension and speaking skills, because I did not have time to create an assessment tool, I did feel the silent period helped my students become more attuned to listening for key words and increased their receptive skills for listening for key words. I also believe the break of silent period allowed my students to relax and overcome their speaking anxieties. Finally, I feel (or felt) the silent period helped my students become better language learners in the end. (Note: Since I decided to continue my studies to learn Japanese when I got home to America, I have found that when I am doing my lessons a silent period does help me learn my lesson faster and memorize the new key words faster.)

As I end this essay about my time in Japan and what I learned as a "sensai," or "teacher," in Japan, I want to note here that I am still in contact with some of my advance students I met at Shibaura. And, much to my surprise (as Dunkel stated in her article), these students have decided to improve their English by listening to English radio programs, watching English speaking TV shows, and going to English only movies (Dunkel, 437). They also have decided they want to visit America and other English speaking countries like England. One of my students got so excited about learning English and improving his English that he spent a month at the University of California at Irvine during his winter break.

(To end this article/essay on one of my teaching experiences in Japan, I think it's fair to say "Not bad for a minority male teacher who was on the verge of walking away from teaching, that is before I went overseas to teach. The sad, or bad, news is that I finally gave up on my dream to be a California Junior College tenured professor because I got the notion I was not welcomed as an "English" professor in this setting. After I was offered a job with the Federal Government, I decided this article was a good way to end an elusive childhood dream.)

Reverie

By Reggie Cornejo

What is it that makes dream?
Is it candle light dinners, or a soft setting sun?
Could be your life, or is it a dream?
Yes, picnic for two, or just having fun?
When is it real? Who is it for?
Could be your time for seeing the moon;
But is it just so, or is it just more?
Just more of this that happened to soon;
I saw a man who lost it all too;
He had the moon, but not in his spoon.
He found the dream, but it fell off the spoon.
That's why he cries as he looks at the moon.
That's why he drives and looks for the sun:
Forgetting too soon that it fell off his spoon!

(I wrote this poem during my undergraduate studies. I don't really know why I wrote it, or what I am saying, but I liked it so much that I decided to save it and see if it grew on me. As you can see, I never threw it out, so I guess I do like it, but, I have yet to figure out what my sub-conscious is trying to say to me.)

The Native

Mother Earth

The Wukchumne Spirits of Rocky Hill

By Reg. Barroso Two Stones

(I decided to include this story/article in this book because it has all of the makings of an out of this world experience and some strange occurrences that I feel can not be explained. I hope my readers will agree with me and enjoy this story.)

The Native

Mother Earth

The Wukchumne Spirits of Rocky Hill

By Reg. Barroso Two Stones

W E ARE PERCHED ATOP THE dome of Rocky Hill (called "Chahka Shahna" or live Oak Place by the local Yokoda Native Americans) scanning the bare ridge sloping to the north from the highest portion of Rocky Hill in Yokoda and Wuckchumne territory, and looking for signs of indigenous life. I want to note that Rocky Hill is found due east of the city of Exeter, California in the San Joaquin Valley.

On this warm winter day, just before noon, we see that there is no wildlife to see anywhere. All we see are rows of four-hundred thousand dollar homes on lots that begin in the mid-thirty thousands according to a sign near this dome. Still, although the tribes are long gone and most of the wild game is too, a spiritual quality permeates this sacred mountain; a spirituality so strong, it has made Mike Edwards and his family believers of the Native American spirits that are said to inhabit this mountain.

According to Mike Edwards, the spirits of the Wukchumne and Yokoda tribes still live and dwell on this place called Rocky Hill. Edwards said that after his parents bought their home located at the base of Rocky Hill that is near hundreds of boulders with Native American paintings on their walls, they discovered the house had been built on an old Wukchumne burial sight. "That's when the strange things started to happen," recalled Edwards.

The strange events Edwards was talking about included the mysterious death of all of their dogs, the unexplained smell of decay in certain sections of their home, and a rash of bad luck that dated back to the day the family moved into the house. The scary part of these events, according to Edwards, was that these examples were just a few of the many strange occurrences his family had to endure.

To explain his examples, Edwards added the most unusual experience he had was what he felt was a visit from a Native American spirit he decided to call Dog-Face. The visit, according to Edwards, happened just after he decided to leave the home to escape the "spirits." "I had moved to Fresno because I was tired of dealing with the supernatural occurrence," added Edwards. "But one night, as I slept, I woke up and was visited by what I guess was a Wukchumne spirit," said Edwards. "He had the head of a dog (Edward's basically said it looked a lot like the Egyptian God Anubis.), and the body of a man," added Edwards.

As Edwards continued, he added that this spirit told him, "his people had made us the caretakers of the hill and the burial sight, and that I had to go back home." As I watched Edwards tell his story, I could tell he was being sincere, so I listened as Edwards added, "The strangest thing about the whole thing is that my little sister told our mother that she saw me outside her window (some 65 miles away) on the night I had the dream,"

Edwards also said that when he woke up the next day his head and scalp had razor like cuts all over his scalp. He speculated that the cuts happened when the spirit stroked his hair during the time he was with the spirit.

The Edwards family noted that their house had been built by the inventor of steam shovel that was used to build the Panama Canal. According to the family, when this gentleman sold the house, he didn't bother to tell anyone about the Native remains that had been dug up and reburied when the house's foundation had been poured. When the house was sold to the Edwards, the previous owners passed on the tradition by not telling the Edwards anything about the Indian remnants either. The Edwards learned of the house's history from a local Wukchumne tribal member.

"We should have known there was something wrong with the house when we started finding all of the Indian paintings on the rocks and the pounding holes all over the rocks," concluded Edwards.

Before I end this article, I want to note that records show the rocks near the backyard of the Edward's home are covered with grinding holes. There is also a place known prayer rock just fifty yards northeast of their house. Since I was curious about the drawings on the rocks, I asked if they would show me where to look for them. I was directed up a small incline with huge boulders all over this area, and I want to add that I immediately found myself among huge rocks covered with small and large drawings that I can only describe as Native American caveman looking like pictures drawn on the rocks. I later learned that according to the National Conservancy, the main tribal burial sight is just east of Edward's house, an area Edwards and his family said they had planned to develop before their ancient supernatural discovery.

(This article was published in the Native Magazine in the Mother Earth section of the magazine in 1993. I decided to use the article in my book because the topic is both strange and has that "believe it or not tone to it." I hope my readers enjoyed this article. Note: While my assistant and I were walking among the drawings on Prayer Rock, a car came by playing the radio so loud we could hear it on the hill, and before we could turn to see what idiot was disturbing the spiritual moment of our visit (I had brought white sage to bless the spirits and thank them for allowing us to visit this sacred Area.), we heard a loud pop and then the car's motor died and it never started again. We left the poor slobs who had evidently angered the spirits to their troubles and drove away the other way. We figured the spirits were in control and we didn't want to encroach on their territory.)

The Pain

By Reggie Cornejo

The children laugh and play
A Dragon bleeds in time
The tide rolled out today
His hide as green as lime
Where once the spring returned
Dark colors cast their shade
His blood no longer churned
The men begin to spade
The lizard moves in pain
Though man will never care
It slowly starts to rain
The wizard comes to share
Nobody seems to care
A tear released in pain
The tide goes out to sea
It still begins to rain
A child is left alone
The garden fills with thorns
The wizard turns to stone
A world is left to mourn

(This poem was published in the California State University, Bakersfield's 1992/1993 Edition of Orpheus, CSUB's annual literary journal. I was doing my graduate work at CSUB when I was honored by having another one of my poems published in this journal that publishes works written by professors, current students, and past students. I decided to not use punctuations in this poem so the reader could decide where to stop, slow down, and move on as he or she read it.)

Ventura County Reporter

Art and Culture Section

Oh, Give me a Home

Where the Buffalo roam—at least
the ones saved from Slaughter

By Reginaldo Cornejo

(I felt this story/article was worth including in this book because of the kind act
the two brothers had decided to commit without any idea they were going to get
the kind of recognition I gave them in this story. If I helped them in anyway, I feel
honored to have had a part in supporting their cause. I hope my readers will enjoy
this little story.)

The two buffalos graze on some straw as they enjoy their new and safe home. The Guzman brothers, in my book, are real heroes because they came to the rescue of two innocent beasts. I think this is a better answer than the one that was shown in the movie that used the song, "Bless the Beast and the Children."

Ventura County Reporter

Art and Culture Section

Oh, Give me a Home

Where the Buffalo roam—at least the
ones saved from Slaughter

By Reginaldo Cornejo

(This article was published July 24, 2003 in the Ventura County Reporter while I was working in the area as a junior college part-time professor at both Moorpark College and Santa Barbara City College. I happened to be driving by a small farm when I noticed the two buffalos in a pen just off the highway. Being Native American, I had to find out why this farm had these two beautiful animals on their farm, and well, here is the story.)

SOME PEOPLE RESCUE CATS AND dogs, but I learned that brothers Lupe and Brian Guzman of Ventura County rescue North American Buffalos, or bison. And as I spoke to the Guzman brothers, I learned that eight of the large and wooly creatures currently reside at the brother's farm that is found on Telegraph Road near Rancho Sespe. All of these magnificent beasts were saved from the slaughter house according to the brothers.

The results of their first rescue mission were a male and female pair of bison from Chino, California that were the ones I saw just off the highway, and these two beasts were the reason I stopped. The first thing I noticed were that the buffalos were enjoying a large reinforced pen that had plenty of shaded areas, plenty of food, and plenty of water, a far cry from the accommodations these two animals shared just before the Guzman brothers saved them from their grisly fate.

When I asked Brian if the animals were being raised to eat, he smiled and said, "No! They are like pets to us. When we got these two in the pen, they were in pretty bad shape, so we treated them for what ever was wrong with them and helped them get healthy."

As I watched the two large bison graze, Brian told me about his family's interest and respect for these indigenous American Icons they had saved— an icon, I want to add, so important to North American tribal nations that in 1992 several Indian tribes created the InterTribal Bison Cooperative (ITBC). The cooperative's mission is simple: "To establish healthy buffalo populations on tribal lands and re-establish hope for Indian people."

I should note that according to records and history at one time there were millions of bison roaming North America, but in the 1800s, the United States Government and European settlers recognized how deeply Indian tribes relied on the hardy and nomadic bison, and so began the systematic destruction of the herds in order to weaken and subjugate the Western Tribal Nations. The slaughter of over 60 million bison left only a few hundred by the turn of the century, and since Native Americans had a symbiotic relationship with the iconic animals, their numbers also declined as many tribes starved to death on U.S. Government controlled reservations.

Whether you are vegetarian or a carnivore, you can probably understand how Brian and Lupe Guzman felt the day they saw the two bison as they awaited their fate in the slaughter house. As my readers can see, the European capitalist idea of using the North American Buffalo as a commodity is now being carried into the 21st Century, and this fact, as I learned is being fueled by a burgeoning market for buffalo meat. As Skip Sayers, the President of the American Bison Association said, "It doesn't take rocket scientist to figure out the advantage [of raising buffalo for commercial use]. I would do well to get 85 cents a pound for cattle, but I can get $1.50 to $1.75 per pound for buffalo."

To be politically correct, the ITBC admitted that some tribes raise their bison to sell, or for their subsistence and cultural use, but the ITBC added these activities are conducted independently by various tribes, each of which allegedly slaughters them according to tribal traditions.

Lloyd Dewey, a 71 year old North American Arapaho, described one of these tribal traditions in this manner: "Our bison are butchered with stone and elk antler tools (no steel knives), the joints are broken with heavy stones and nothing that is part of the bison is ever wasted." According to Dewey, a full grown bison/buffalo can be butchered by a tribe within and hour: "This method of preparation makes it a sacred event. The buffalo is also thanked for its life during the preparation," concluded Dewey.

I want to note the ITBC is a non profit 501 (C) (3) concern that currently has 42 member tribes with a collective heard of over 8,000 buffalo. The organization remains committed to re-establishing bison herds on Indian lands in a manner that promotes cultural enhancement, spiritual revitalization, ecological restoration and economic development for tribes across the American Nation.

While they harbor no cultural imperative to save the North American buffalo, the Guzman brothers are doing their own part to support this once-dying breed by buying and tending to the rescued bison simply because they find these magnificent animals entertaining—and too proud an animal to end up as ground meat on someone's table: "We felt they deserved a better life," says Brian Guzman.

This October, the public will have free access to the Guzman farm to view the bison; the brothers are also growing pumpkins for Halloween, and to make the visit to the farm more fun, shoppers will be allowed to visit these lumbering charming giants while browsing for prospective Jack-O-Lantern pumpkins.

And if you can't help but be curious about the taste of buffalo meat, I suggest visitors/vacationers head down to Winchester's Grill and Saloon on Main Street in Ventura, California (Note: Since this story was published back in 2003, I can't verify if these choices are still available in 2019.), where vacationers might be able to pick up a buffalo burger and fries for about seven dollars. Enjoy.

A Word to the Wise

By a "Wise Person"

"The innovator makes enemies of all those who

Prospered under the old order, and only lukewarm

Support is forthcoming from those who would

Prosper under the new order."

A word from the wise

(I found this statement by an anonymous writer so enthralling and unique that I decided to use it here to introduce my next article, instead of one of my works. I felt it fit here better than any thing I had written.)

Hispanic Outlook in Higher Education

Hispanic Scholar in Hong Kong Feels the Heat

By Reginaldo Cornejo

(Since the news in 2019 appears to be constantly show casing the growing trade problems between the Chinese and U.S. Government, I thought this article/story I wrote back in 2002 fit in nicely in this book. So, I now present a reminder to my fellow Americans that China and her Communist Government are not always what they appear to be when the cameras are on them.)

This photo was taken from the steps of the Window of the World theme park. In the background my readers can see the skyline of this fast growing city that was once just a small quiet city. To the right of the tall apartment complexes in the background, I want my readers to notice the shorter building with the white pillars in front of the building. This building is where I gave my presentation.

Hispanic Outlook in Higher Education

Hispanic Scholar in Hong Kong Feels the Heat

By Reginaldo Cornejo

(Published March 11, 2002 in the Hispanic Outlook in Higher Education. I wrote this article right after I came home from my "business" trip to Hong Kong and Shenzhen because it had been such a scary and strange trip. This article appears in this book with the gracious permission of the Hispanic Outlook in Higher Education. I wish to thank Suzanne Isa-Lopez for her kindness and professionalism.)

AS AN AMERICAN WITH HISPANIC and North American Indian roots, and one who has left the U.S. soil on many occasions to travel and work overseas, I have slipped in and out of immigration check points in other countries with few or any problems. But had anyone hidden in my suitcase on my scholarly trip to Hong Kong (China) and mainland China (Schenzhen) during the month of March, they might have noticed several "James Bond" type close encounters this man of color had with Chinese Government officials and some I would call special operatives.

When I arrived at Hong Kong's International Airport and queued up for immigration processing, the immigration officers made me stand in line longer after they found out I was an American educator who had just been to Japan. After being processed, I heard two camera clicks as I walked by some officers standing near the exit gate.

"I estimate that most of the immigration and government officials I ran into in Hong Kong were not your typical government Employees." (Hispanic Outlook In Higher Education highlight)

My telephone line at my hotel was not very private. I can say this because on several occasions I heard noises that were not made by my phone pal or me. And, although I was there on education business, I was asked to travel to Shenzhen (mainland China) by train to deliver a speech at a People's Hall in mainland China. This presentation was set up by some international center (group). After I made my presentation, I was to be given a tour of several Chinese landmarks, tourist stops, and dinner.

However, a strange event happened to me while I was waiting in the town of Kowlon for my train to Shenzhen. When I went to buy a ticket to Shenzhen on the Kowlon-Canton Railway, I was asked for my passport and then asked if I was an American. I said, "Yes." The train officials then told me where I had to wait for my train, but while I was waiting I started to feel uneasy because I was sent to an isolated island, and the locals had not. I then walked over to where the locals had gathered to wait, but I felt I was being watched. When I looked around, I found a young man with a portable video camera taping my every move.

Although I still went to mainland China and did my presentation, this event put me on the defensive, so when I was asked to spend the night in mainland China, I kindly declined and went back to Hong Kong and the safety of my hotel.

I should note that although the isolated and uncomfortable episodes with spy-like situations scared me (these types of encounters appear to be new to Hong Kong), but in reality they are very common in mainland China. I can say this because nosy and overaggressive officials are hardly a new phenomenon on the Communist side of mainland China (This was not in my original story, but I want to note the news in 2019 shows that now that Communist China controls Hong Kong, it is tightening its control of Hong Kong's citizens.). Virtually everyone in Hong Kong that I came in contact with warned me to be "careful" when I went to Shenzhen for my visit and speech. My hotel front office person told me to let her know when I returned so she could inform her manager.

To prove my point as to how dangerous it can be for foreigners when they enter Communist China, in his article, "Arrests in China make scholars reluctant to visit," Mark Landler quoted X. L. Ding (an expert in Chinese economy and legal systems at Hong Kong University of Science and Technology) as saying, "It is not wise to go [to mainland China] now because we don't know what's permissible and what's not." Ding added later, "People got into trouble before, but the reasons were quite clear. Now it's not clear at all [why]" (San Francisco Chronicle, April 22, 2001, P D3).

I agree with Mr. Ding's observation. I estimate that most of the immigration and government officials I ran into in Hong Kong were not your typical government employees. They all appeared to be more operative or security type personnel. Those on the street who photographed and video taped me also appeared to be trained well. I believe the only reason I was able to notice these men and women working these jobs was that I have been an investigative reporter for over nine years (before I became a teacher), and I guess I can say I get a gut feeling when things are not right.

Not only have these strange spy-like events increased in China and Hong Kong, but the severity of these events has also increased. A month before I arrived in Hong Kong/China, Landler wrote in his article, "Li Shaomin, an American citizen who teaches business at City University of Hong Kong was detained February 25 by security agents while visiting a friend in mainland China." Landler also noted that China had not confirmed the report that was filed by Li's wife.

Other visitors who have found trouble in mainland China include author Wu Jiamin, a U. S. citizen arrested on April 8 (2001) for suspicion of spying on behalf of Taiwan; Tan Guangguang, a Chinese citizen with U. S. residency who was arrested for suspicion of divulging state secrets; Gao Zhan (American University in Washington researcher), a Chinese citizen with U. S. residency who was charged with espionage on behalf of Taiwan; and Liu Yaping, another Chinese citizen with U. S. residency who was charged with fraud, tax evasion, and divulging state secrets (NBC News Webtv.net, May 22, 2001).

I should note none of the aforementioned visitor come from Hispanic or American Indian roots, but believe me, I don't look White or Asian, so if I was a marked man, then any American going to mainland China should be aware that China's distrust for Americans has gone up since our presidential elections, and any educator who visits mainland China or Hong Kong should be aware of these new developments. (Note: Although this article was published in 2002, I still feel that China's government should not be trusted by educators entering mainland China in 2019.)

Unfortunately this type of diplomacy is not good for higher education or for China's educational system, which is just now starting to reach out to English-speaking countries for academic exchanges—or the reason I was in Hong Kong and traveled to Schenzhen. Addressing this topic, Landler noted that the "rising tensions" would hurt Hong Kong and mainland China "because it will discourage scholars from doing fieldwork in mainland China." He quoted David Zweig, and expert on rural China at the University of Science and Technology, by adding this statement, "People are going to put lecture tours on hold, [and] the flow of information will dry up" (Landler, P. D3).

From my observation, studies and contacts with China's people and its government, I believe that both China and America are responsible for the tensions between these two world powers, and America appears to be the one with the most to gain and the least to lose in this political game of saber rattling.

So, do I believe China should be protective and suspicious of educators like me coming to Hong Kong and mainland China? No. And I agree with most experts who say that helping developing countries like China expand their trade borders not only helps China, but America's large and small businesses and our economy too. You don't have to have an MBA in Business to arrive at this conclusion. In fact, the idea of finding new products in Shenzhen was one other reason I accepted the invitation to go to mainland China. Why take the risk? For business and a chance to find new products in a city designated as a Special Economic Zone (SEZ) by the Chinese government.

I want to close this article by adding that Shenzhen is an industrial city in the Guangdon Province, so much of the travel to and from this city is for business. Many skyscrapers have shot up in Shenzhen now that it has been designated a Special Economic Zone. Since I had an escort, I had few problems finding my way around this city that appears to have a new building going up on every corner. I also had very few problems finding things to do in Shenzhen because it has many tourist attractions.

The tourist attractions don't compare in size or creativity of California's theme parks, but they aren't bad. I had the pleasure of spending the evening at Window of the World theme park where I was treated to a few rides, a colorful and live show, a dinner, and a fireworks display. Although I was offered a place to spend the night in Shenzhen, and my business trip had gone well, I decided to listen to my little voice and leave while I could on my own accord. I think it was a good idea and choice because you never know what might happen in mainland China.

Blind Faith

A wizard hides in solitude.

The wolf may howl at night.

Depends upon your attitude;

The earth may hold him tight.

The rain will come tomorrow.

An hour kills the light;

Another chance to borrow,
while a baby cries at night.

The wizard shames the oracle;

Can white turn into gray?

Yes, when faith rots in a grave.

(This poem came out of my mind one day while I was preparing for a test in one of my college courses. I have no idea why it came to me, but since it wrote itself, I decided to write it down and save it for the future. I have decided to include it in this book. I don't know why.)

The Native

Pow-Wow Trail

Chumash Dolphin Dancers
make Ojai Day '93 Special

By Reg. B Two Stones

(I wrote this article/story for <u>The Native</u> magazine back in 1993 because I felt the community of Ojai deserved to be recognized for including the original inhabitants of the Ojai Valley in their celebration of this unique and calm bucolic city and area. As I watched the dancers perform Native dances, I was happy to see how much the crowd showed their appreciation for these local Chumash Dolphin dancers and the Native Americans of this area.)

The Native

Pow-Wow Trail

Chumash Dolphin Dancers make
Ojai Day '93 Special

By Reg. B Two Stones

GENTLE WARM BREEZES AND PUFFY, thick clouds roamed through the Ojai Valley while a lively group of Chumash Dolphin Dancers entertained a large and appreciative crowd at the Ojai Day '93 celebration on October 9.

The dancers, dressed in their traditional ceremonial Native American outfits, performed for the big crowd at 11 A.M. on the main stage that is called the Libby Bowl in Ojai. I want to note the Libby Bowl, for anyone not familiar with the city of Ojai, is a Hollywood Bowl-type structure that provides a great forum for any performance requiring a bond between the audience and the performers.

The emcees for the dancers were Julie Tumamait and Michael Ward, two local Chumash Historians. The two Chumash historian emcees had the crowd clinging to their seats as they explained the dances and introduced the many dancers on the stage. A special touch was also added by Tony Romero, the head of the dancing group, who told several Chumash stories that revealed Chumash folklore and mythology.

According to Craig Walker, the events coordinator, this year marked the second appearance of the Dolphin Dancers. "The Chumash Tribal Dancers were asked to participate because they're so much a part of the history of the Ojai Valley," said Walker. "We try to include as much of the local culture as possible on Ojai Day," added Mr. Walker. As we talked, Walker also added that Ojai is a Chumash name that means the "Valley of the Moon."

Although "Ojai" is a Chumash word, I want to note that there are several tales about the meaning of the word "Ojai." Another story about the word "Ojai" claims that the word came from a tribe of Native Americans who crossed the Bering Straits and wandered around the Southwest for thousands of years. When the tribe came to the Valley, they named it "Ojai," or "the nest," for the way the mountains cradled the valley of Ojai. And thus, the tribe finally settled in the Ojai Valley.

The color of both of these short tales shows why the Chumash tribe is regarded as a cornerstone of the history of the Ojai Valley. It also explains why Native American artifacts dating back over 6,000 years B.C. have been found throughout the valley.

Travelers who have the opportunity to visit the city of Ojai should not miss the city's Museum. I add this information because the city's Museum has a large array of artifacts such as Native American bead work, shell necklaces, axes, hoes, spears, arrow points, pottery and basketry. A display portraying the Chumash culture and a toad effigy (one of the oldest three-dimensional art objects ever discovered in North America) are among the more interesting exhibits.

According to Ojai history, the tradition of Ojai Day was started back in 1917 to honor Edward Drummond Libby. Libby gave the City of Ojai its most cherished landmarks, which include the Ojai Arcade, Post Office Tower, Libby Park, Ojai Library, Arbolada tract, Catholic Chapel, Oaks Hotel, Ojai Valley Inn, and the Ojai Avenue Pergola. History tell us the "Ojai Day" event died out in the late 1920s but was revived in 1991 by Craig Walker and the Ojai Day Committee to commemorate the renovation of the Arcade. Walker stated that Ojai Day is only celebrated every other year because, "The event takes a full year to plan, and another year to hold it." We can only hope that this holiday's revival will be around for a long time to come.

Ode to a Special Teacher

By D. J.

(Note: I am not going to introduce my final short essay/story with one of my poems. Instead, I am going to use a poem that was written by a very special person that tried to stop me from giving up on my dream of being a college professor, when I decided to quit and go in a different direction. This poem I think works well with my final essay because in this essay I again return to my teaching ways and educate my fellow Americans on what it means to be a Native American in the 21st Century, and how we survive.)

Their Hearts have died

The students cried

There is no light within;

But through their prayers

And one who cared,

A candle burns for them;

Its flame is bright

And full of life

A glow, it draws so many,

And gathers near

Those less in fear and

Sends them on their journey.

The Medicine Wheel of the Native American

By Reg. B Two Stones

(I wrote this essay for a friend of mine that wanted to understand why I wore a medicine wheel and a an eagle feather on my hat every day. I felt the best way to teach him about my people was to put my thoughts on the topic in writing. I now offer my thoughts on this topic to my fellow Americans.)

The Medicine Wheel of the Native American

By Reg. B Two Stones

W HEN PEOPLE FIRST MEET ME, they are often caught off guard by the colorful medicine wheel and large eagle feather I wear on my baseball style caps. Some of these people ask me if it's a peace sign or a charm for good luck. After a short introduction about my heritage (that I'm Native American), I usually try to explain that both of these items are just part of my heritage, my culture, and my people's philosophy of life. I then tell them I wear these items because they both remind me of who I am, and these items both help me cope with being a Native American in 21st Century modern America, a modern America that to this day does not understand my people and our way of life. In the end, these brief encounters often appear to raise my questions than provide answers, so I decided to write this short essay and try to explain the medicine wheel and our connection with eagle feathers.

I guess the best way to begin this kind of discussion is on a historical note, so here is some light history for my readers about my people's ways. I want to start by saying that Native Americans, in the past, were often portrayed or accused of being non-religious savages. To see how prevalent Native Americans were stereotyped or portrayed as heathen savages, all we have to do is watch a few old, or early, western movies from the early days of Hollywood. But since this essay is not about these movies, I want to also point out that when Hollywood, the U.S. Government, or the early media wanted to show how America had converted these savages to the Christian faith and made them "civilized," they would often show my ancestors wearing European style clothing, sporting shorter hair, and wearing hats. Unfortunately for these so called Christian converters, little did these people and writers know that deep down in the souls of these alleged converted savages there often beat a heart that was already religious to a point. Yes, some were more religious than others, but basically my people already knew the creator and they followed the Native American discipline of the "Red Road of life."

First I want to say, the medicine wheel, the eagle feather, and the pipe are all symbols to Native American of how they are supposed to live and walk the "Red Road of Life." These symbols of life are (I guess I can say) guides that help, or allow, my people stay on the road that leads them to becoming "human beings" in the eyes of the rest of the tribal members. To tell the truth, before any white man set foot on the Americas, I can honestly say that most Native American tribes had accepted the ancient ways of self-discipline that were tied to Grandfather, or the creator, and the "Red Road."

I now say that I am no different from my ancestors before me. I was raised by my grandmother and family to know the way of walking the "Red Road" that leads to becoming a good human being, and in these modern times being a good Christian. Thanks to the symbolism and philosophy of life that is found at the center of the medicine wheel, I now try to always walk my own Red Road, like a good Indian and modern day Christian. And as I walk my Red Road, I carry the charms or symbols known as the medicine wheel and the Lord's cross to remind me of my commitment to try to live a life that does not include lying, cheating, stealing, or sinning to the best of my ability. But the wheel's philosophy also includes the words that tell me not to drink the white man's alcohol (firewater), take drugs, and gamble carelessly, which are the white man's crutches and vices that lead to dependence as a way of life. Therefore, I walk the "Red Road." It is a good road, and it is the medicine wheel way, that if my fellow Christian brothers look closely is rich in many Christian values.

So what does the medicine wheel look like? Well, the medicine wheel is a wheel or circle with a cross in the center of the circle. The cross represents the four directions of a compass. The medicine wheel, I want to add, also has two more directions that are not as obvious to a non-native: The first direction is above the wheel when it is laid on its side and this direction is Heaven. The second direction is found in the center of the wheel which is considered below the Heavens, and this direction is where Mother Earth lies for my people. I want to point out to my readers that Heaven and Earth are considered the center of our Native American philosophy. Having pointed this key fact, I want to add that since Native Americans consider the center of the medicine wheel the center of Native American philosophy, when we give thanks to the creator for any blessing we might have received or are praying for, we raise the ceremonial pipe (called the peace pipe by whites and now some modern Native Americans) we turn in each direction of the compass

(North, East, West, and South) and pray in the reverence and philosophy that is found and attached to these items.

As my people point the pipe to the west, my people find a place that helps them look inside themselves, or their inner soul. In this place my people examine their strengths and their weaknesses. In this place they stop to reflect on Grandfather or the Creator. A Creator that the New Testament says all men find because "For the grace of God that bringeth salvation hath appeared to all men" (Titus 2:11). Although my people had never read the New Testament, as my readers can see, they already knew there was one God that ruled everything on this earth. So my readers should understand and see, the teachings of God/Jesus or Grandfather were not foreign to my people. My people loved and worshipped the Creator long before the New Testament or Bible had been brought to this land. And, they had (and have) always respected his creations, and they never abused God's gifts. My readers should also see and understand my people also knew of God's way of life or teachings. My people knew if they followed the "Red Road," or in a round about way, followed the Lord's teachings, they would be able to fight their weaknesses and shortcomings.

I guess I can say the West was like a Church in their heart to my people. I say this because in the West my people found a place of solitude. This place, or the West, is a place for the soul, a place for contemplation, and a place for prayer. A place my people can visit, but not get lost in. This place taught my people that all things must be done in moderation. In this place, we learned that prayer to the Creator (God) was good, but that chanting and isolation from the world was not good for us. Finally the West taught my people (and me) that they must pray for themselves and for others, then they must go out and share their lives and gifts with others.

As my people point the "Ceremonial pipe" towards the North, they find a place of learning. In this place, my people learn moderation through knowledge. They also learn that material things are good, but they can't provide happiness or peace of mind. My people also learn that knowledge is good, but the thirst for knowledge can sometimes consume the soul and become a disease. In the Northern part of the Medicine Wheel, my people find, like the white man, a place to pray for guidance to help them build strong families and communities. My people believe in strong family values, and they pray for temperance to avoid becoming too proud, selfish, or self-centered. Like the New Testament (in the Bible) teaches the world, the philosophy of the Medicine Wheel in the North offers the same message to my people, "Love not the world, neither the things that are in the world. If any man love the world, the love of the father (or creator) is not in him" (John 1:15). As people who love Grandfather and his teachings (or God), my people and I believe and pray for no less.

When my people point the Ceremonial Pipe to the East, my people and I find the Native American's place of Wisdom. Here, my people find a way to use our gained wisdom for the good of the people. We learn there are many people who learn facts and figures, but they never help their people. My people also learn that intelligence does not teach you wisdom or the difference between good and evil. We also learn that intelligence does not create good judgment qualities. My readers should see and learn that the way of Medicine Wheel teaches my people that wisdom and not knowledge is the key to intelligence. My people understand in this place that wisdom can change a fool into a sage. We understand that wisdom is good for our people, and it can be used to light the way for us.

As my people raise the ceremonial pipe to the final compass point that is the South, my people find a good place. It is a place where my people find feelings, love, compassion, pity, tenderness, sympathy, and the way of becoming a "human being." I am a member of the Great Apache Nation of human beings. I am a member of the Mescalero, Lipan, and Navajo tribes on my mother's side of the family. My life as a member of these strong and proud people is a good life. In this place of the compass point known as the South, my people become Inde or "The People." From this area we learn to love and be loved. My people learn from this place that a person must learn to love correctly, for love can both help and hurt people. If a person loves foolishly, they will waste their love on empty love. My people know from this place that a person must love himself before he or she can love others. So, my people know that when we love, we must discern between good and bad love. In the end, the Southern point of the compass has always taught my people that love has the power to create or destroy, so we must be careful with the power that is love.

Before I end the discussion of the Medicine Wheel, I now want to cover the final two points found on the Medicine Wheel. The first of the two final points of the Medicine Wheel is found above the Medicine Wheel when it is laid on its side (as opposed to hanging it from a lanyard or chain). This place or direction is the Heavens, or Heaven. In this direction, my people find the power and medicine to live in the old ways, or walking the "Red Road." The old ways include wearing our hair long, because as Native Americans often say, "An Indian is nothing without his hair." The old ways also includes wearing the Medicine Wheel as part of our everyday regalia. These acts of heritage to the Native American are the way of the "Red Road." Since today's Native Americans have become a part of main stream Americana, many Natives believe in the way of a Christian Life because we believe it is good medicine. Since my people have always lived in harmony with the Great Creator, accepting the teachings of the Bible is a good way of life. The only part that confuses many of my people (and me) is that although we know God's way, as taught in the Bible, is a good life, why does the white man continue to drink heavily, divorce their mates, steal from each other, cheat each other, lie to each other, and finally commit sins unto mankind and Mother Earth?

My people do not know if religion is the answer to happiness, but since we are not savages, as we were once labeled, we feel that embracing the God's way is a good way because it keeps us from turning to the white man's vices. My people find a good place in the Heavens of the Great Creator so for now we will continue to live and walk the "Red Road." If my people walk the Red Road, we know that when our time to die comes, we will be able to say, "It is a good day to die," and not ask for more time to make amends.

The final point of the Medicine Wheel is the center of the wheel (when it is laid on its side). In the center of the Medicine Wheel we find Mother Earth. To my people, Mother Earth is not here for us to own or abuse. Mother Earth belongs to all of the inhabitants of the world, both human and beast. As the care takers of the Earth, my people have always been committed to not abusing the Earth and making sure that they never take more than they need. My people have always lived as one with the Earth and believed that no one owned the Earth. My people felt this way because the one fact they knew was that the life of a "human being" (or Native American) was like a full circle, or that "the People (or Inde) were born to die." Life was a full circle that could never be broken or escaped from. My people believed that since we were just another creature living on the Creator's Earth "the People" were connected to the earth just as the trees, clouds, rocks, grasses, water, and wind were all part of the earth or connected to the earth. So, if mankind continues to destroy the Earth's resources, mankind will soon become extinct like many of the flora and fauna that are disappearing from the earth on a daily basis. The earth is talking to mankind because she needs help, if mankind will listen. She is saying she is sick and on life support, and if mankind and her governments do not change their ways in the near future, Mother Earth will soon die and so will mankind.

Can mankind and Native Americans save Mother Earth? I don't have the answer, but I will say that mankind is running out of time. These are the words of my people. These are the teachings of my people. Let those who want to learn listen. Tah-in-hoon-ay-ish-lee. Tak-she-Nah-Kee-Teesh. Translation: I am a friend; I am Two Stone.

Ode to the Day

By RB Two Stones Cornejo

I woke up yesterday,

To find it very new;

Though it was today,

It wasn't very new;

Lived it like a haze;

Did it once before;

Wandered in a daze;

Wandered through a door;

Perhaps it wasn't yesterday?

Or, was it long ago?

Woke up here today;

Yet, I lived it long ago.

(Although this poem does not appear to have much to do with the final work I offer my readers in this book, I feel it works here because the topic of the poem deals with loss of time and days that slip away and die like my teaching career slipped away and died before my eyes.)

(Note: My final written work that I am going to include in this book was researched, written, and published for the use of Oxnard Junior College in 1998 to help the school complete its self-study plan that was needed to continue to meet the required accreditation standards for all California Junior Colleges. I offered my services because I had just completed a one year full-time non-tenured teaching contract at Oxnard College, and I felt I could help this school meet the dead- line that was fast approaching to present its self-study findings. I am presenting it here so my readers will see California Junior College professor/teachers are asked to do more than just teach their courses that are assigned to them each Semester. I hope this sample of my work will help the public see the many hats California's Junior College Professors wear and the abilities I offered my students when they found themselves in my classes.)

Accreditation Research for Oxnard College

A Self-Study and Institutional Plan

By Reginaldo Cornejo, Research Analyst

Published by Cornejo Publishing Company

Copyright 1998 by Cornejo Publishing Company

(Note: The following research sample is from the Introduction of the research study I presented to Oxnard College's Accreditation committee that introduced various "Outlook Papers" and Chapters.)

To: Steve Arvizu, Carmen Guerro-Calderon, Dennis Cabral, & Committees

From: Reginaldo Cornejo, Research Analyst, CEO Cornejo Publications

Date: August 5, 1998

Subject: Strategies, Research, and Facts Needed for Oxnard College Accreditation/Master Education Plan and Faculty Use Plan

Accreditation Research for Oxnard College's Master Education Plan

Introduction

As I mentioned at the Accreditation Team's meeting, I honestly believe that this Accreditation team and current Oxnard College Administration is ready, willing, and able to revise, or create, a solid Accreditation Self-Study and Master Education Plan that will serve as a guide for on going improvement that will carry the college into the Millennium. As I looked over what the team had done to date (May 1998), however, I noticed many areas where I could help the team improve its function, results, and final presentation. Beyond the issues of selecting team leader and setting up meetings, I was able to help the team bring its study and presentation into sharper focus and tightened up its response for the Accreditation Committee's visit. If you have any questions on the material or information that I have gathered for your team's use, please feel free to call me at my office.

As a result of my initial review of your information and my research, I propose the following course of action that will be explained in my findings and my completed report:

* Conduct a final interview with Steve Arvizu to discuss the overall vision of the presentation and my research's findings. This interview would be conducted within one or two weeks of execution of any payment that is allowed according to your budget.

  * Based on our meetings and further review of your Progress Report (Dated August 15, 1997) on the spring of 1997 activities of the sub-committees for Standards for Accreditation, provided input to you in the form of this written report and all of the Outlook Papers that I have prepared for your use. These tasks were completed during the months of June and July.

*   Provide a complete report of the findings and suggestions needed to enhance OC's workable Master Education Plan and Facilities Use Plan.

   *   Provide support and answers to your questions (limited to the scope of this project) via telephone and e-mail.

The hours used to complete this project were set at 50 hours, as discussed with Co-Chair Carmen Guerro-Calderon. I have since been informed by Ms. Calderon that due to some financial problems at Oxnard College the school might not have the money to pay my fee for this work. I have, since this time, informed Ms. Calderon that I will provide the finished work even if do not get paid. I will write this unpaid work off as a loss to my publishing company, The Cornejo Publishing Company. If funds are found to be available, I will expect to be paid at the hourly rate I was paid as an instructor of English at Oxnard College. (Please note: This project took 65 hours to complete.) (2019 Note: To my readers of the book "The Will to Write," I was paid when all was said and done by the college for my work.)

I look forward to discussing this completed project with your staff. I know that you will be happy with the final product.

The Problem

As discussed in several meetings (example: 2/6/98 and 2/20/98, etc.), the accreditation committees are behind schedule for this presentation of Oxnard College's Self-Study to the Visiting Accreditation Team. As noted in the Progress Report dated 8-15-97, "much work has been accomplished and survey statements have been submitted...; even so [the team] still [has] more work to complete." This research is intended to not only help this team complete their job, but also make their work easier and help them (and Oxnard College) create a revised Master Education Plan and Facilities Five-Year Master Plan.

Objectives

The research in this project is intended to provide practical assistance to insure the completion and fulfillment of not only the needed Self-Study but also the revision of the Master Education Plan and Facilities Five-Year Master Plan so that Oxnard College can maximize student learning and provide the "Key to effective planning in a streamlined process that focuses on future students' learning needs" ((Planning Resources Guide, 1997). To that end, this research project/study provides samples, working papers, completed research, charts, and suggestions for the implementation and creation of the aforementioned plans.

Recommendations

Planning

Since Oxnard College still does not have a clear or defined planning process for its institutional planning process, this study would like to recommend a "Three-year Rolling Plan" to get "the ball rolling." After two years of working with the process, this plan can then be changed to a "Five-Year Rolling Plan." One word of warning, the author of this paper has found that, from experience, a five-year plan is a bit dated because it's too long for today's fast changing times. The author, that taught me the rolling plan process pointed out the benefits of a rolling plan quite well when he said, "I like the rolling plans rather than fixed one because you change the last or third year of the plan as you make adjustments and generally leave the first two years of the plan intact" (Bobrow, 23). The "Three-Year Rolling Plan" is therefore being updated yearly to accommodate the changes taking place within the environment you are operating in; yet, you will maintain your goals and you will have clear patterns for at least a two-year period.

Note: **Three-Year Rolling Plan: "A process by which you plan three years, and at the end of the first year, you again plan the third year leaving the first and second year intact. In other words, each year, you roll over the first two years and plan the third year" (Bobrow, 23).**

Please see sample below:

Table 1.0 Planning Structure for the "Three-Year Rolling Plan."

Years: 1   2   3   4   5

Plan all Three years

First Year: 1 2 3

Activate Plan

Second Year: Done   1   2   3

Plan Third Year

Third Year: Done   1   2   3

Plan Third Year

Some important observations that the author made known were found in the area of organization. He felt that plans needed to be "flexible, monitored, and frequently analyzed to be useful." According to the author, "Changes should not be made lightly, but made as required. Even if you are operating on the basis of a 'Three-Year Plan,' sometimes you cannot wait for changes to be made in the third year. You have to break into the cycle and make immediate changes. Of course, this should be done only with very careful thought and only for absolutely necessary reasons" (Bobrow, 24).

Working examples of the aforementioned plan: Plan to improve current vocational programs by adding an LVN (Licensed Vocational Nurse) program at OC in 1999. First year would include the creation of the curriculum, hiring the staff, ordering books, marketing the plan, getting local community involvement (hospitals, community at large, business district, etc.), scheduling the facilities to be used, ordering classroom equipment, and developing a marketing plan. Second Year would include the marketing of the program, student enrollment, recruiting both locally and from fringe areas, and planning the expansion of the program. The third year would include a program evaluation from both students and staff, improvement plans, new marketing plans, and if the program is doing well, some new plans for diversification of the program and expansion (offering the prerequisites for RN (Registered Nurse) programs at four year institutions.

Buy In:

In the area of "Buy In," management is reminded that expectancy theory tells us that what would appear to be an obvious expectation—completing the Self-Evaluation Study—is sometimes individualized to a wide variety of sub-expectations: For Example, settling the district's contract problems, negotiations, and family problems to name a few. But there is hope and it comes from Victor Vroom:

"Victor Vroom has helped generations of managers understand the inner workings of expectancy. Vroom points out that expectancy involves three key factors:

1: If you believe that your efforts affects your performance
   (and)
2: If you believe that your performance determines predictable outcomes
   (and)
3: If you believe that you value those outcomes

… …then you will be motivated to expend maximum or near-maximum effort" (Smith, 22).

Here is an Example: In Reggie's case, he first expects that his personal investment of energy (in the form of student retention, tenured track position, personal growth classes, etc.) will affect his performance as an educator. "No one gets a free ride in this world," Reggie likes to say. Second, Reggie expects that his performance will lead to predictable outcomes: He expects to enjoy the benefits of a full-time tenured track position someday. Finally, Reggie knows that he values both financial rewards and the prestige of being a top performer in his fields of writing and education. But, remove any one of Vroom's three components and Reggie's motivation evaporates. So, to motivate Reggie, an employer has to put value into the task at hand—completing the Self-Evaluation Study—because by completing the task, "Reggie will gain visibility as a team player and a person who wants OC to succeed as an institution. This visibility will then increase his prestige as a top educator. In short, we work because we believe, not because we receive...

Mission

After reading the attached Outlook Papers, the Accreditation Committee should understand that our job as educators is more than providing educational opportunities, access to information, and the development of competencies (not that these objectives aren't important); Our mission should also include the job of providing education and training, which will afford our students the choices of either transferring to baccalaureate institutions or leaving Oxnard College ready for the job market. Since our students are the future of both California and the United States, as educators, we should establish standard-based reforms, close partnerships with business, implementation of new technologies, value added accountability measures of school performance, and portfolio and performance-based assessments, so Oxnard College can enhance the economic growth and global competiveness of both the United States and California.

Oxnard College should also be committed to providing and improving its development and remedial education programs and improving and providing a wide range of student services for the successful attainment of their educational and career goals (Note: This is one of OC's strengths.).

OC's Vision for the Future

The following recommendations are made from information that is implied in the attached Outlook Papers. The following themes comprise some recommended visions that OC's committees can use to develop OC's Vision for the Future:

Since the visiting committee commended Oxnard College for "A curricula with an appropriate mixture of basic skills, vocational/technical programs, general education, community services, and transfer programs which provide a range of educational opportunities for a diverse community," (Evaluation Report Oxnard College, 2), Oxnard College should commit to providing flexibility in curriculum and teaching styles, establish a core curriculum based on communication and collaboration; make sure OC faculty are seen as a valuable existing resource and match teaching and learning styles to take into account the skill levels of those being taught.

In the area of delivery and instruction, some groups feel more (still) needs to be done so that the responsibility falls on the entire campus and not student services. Changing demographics and changing economic conditions along with inter-college resource equity issues do not appear to be directly considered in the planning process as drivers of the plan (Evaluation Report Oxnard College, 3), so to that end, Oxnard College should commit to addressing diversity in all forms that include cultural, age, skill levels, origin, and etc. OC should also commit to providing an infusion of diversity awareness and issues into the curriculum without confusing the "benefits of pluralistic multiculturalism over the negative effects of particularistic multiculturalism" (The State of Education, 95). In order to evaluate programs and services, OC should commit to adopt a program review, encourage risk taking in evaluation and assessment, encourage students to conduct self-evaluation, and to conduct evaluation and assessment across all levels of the institution. In the area of community linkages, Oxnard College should commit to continue it articulation efforts with both colleges and high schools, continue to connect on grass roots level with local business and industry, and include community service membership to connect the college to the broader population.

Note: The rest of this report included "Outlook Papers" that covered the following topics: Learning and Teaching Assessment, Facilities Outlook, Fiscal Outlook, Transfer Outlook, Enrollment Outlook, Workforce Outlook, and the Unique Characteristics of Oxnard College. I hope my readers enjoyed reading this report that I completed for Oxnard College and that it helped them see that Junior College Professors wear many hats as employees of local junior colleges. As my readers can see, I loved being a college teacher/professor, but I guess the Lord had a different path that I had to follow because I never became a full-time college teacher.

Printed in the United States
By Bookmasters